New Dayl

CW00673545

Edited by **Gordon Giles** January–April 2025

BRF Ministries

15 The Chambers, Vineyard,
Abingdon OX14 3FE
+44 (0)1865 319700 | brf.org.uk

Bible Reading Fellowship is a charity (233280)
and company limited by guarantee (301324),
registered in England and Wales

ISBN 978 1 80039 356 1
All rights reserved

This edition © Bible Reading Fellowship 2024
Cover image: Baily Lighthouse, Dublin, Ireland by Bhargava Marripati/pexels.com
Editor and contributor photos used with kind permission

Distributed in Australia by:
MediaCom Education Inc, PO Box 610, Unley, SA 5061
Tel: 1 800 811 311 | admin@mediacom.org.au

Distributed in New Zealand by:
Scripture Union Wholesale, PO Box 760, Wellington 6140
Tel: 04 385 0421 | suwholesale@clear.net.nz

Acknowledgements
Scripture quotations marked with the following abbreviations are taken from the version
shown. Where no abbreviation is given, the quotation is taken from the same version as
the headline reference. **NIV**: The Holy Bible, New International Version, Anglicised edition,
copyright © 1979, 1984, 2011 by Biblica. Used by permission of Hodder & Stoughton
Publishers, an Hachette UK company. All rights reserved. 'NIV' is a registered trademark of
Biblica. UK trademark number 1448790. **NRSV** (except 12 and 13 January): the New Revised
Standard Version Updated Edition. Copyright © 2021 National Council of Churches of Christ
in the United States of America. Used by permission. All rights reserved worldwide. The
quotations on 12 and 13 January are taken from the New Revised Standard Version Anglicised
edition, copyright © 1989, 1995 by the Division of Christian Education of the National Council
of the Churches of Christ in the United States of America. Used by permission. All rights
reserved. **RSV**: the Revised Standard Version of the Bible, copyright © 1946, 1952, 1971 by the
Division of Christian Education of the National Council of the Churches of Christ in the United
States of America. Used by permission. All rights reserved.

A catalogue record for this book is available from the British Library

Printed and bound in the UK by Zenith Media NP4 0DQ

Suggestions for using *New Daylight*

Find a regular time and place, if possible, where you can read and pray undisturbed. Before you begin, take time to be still and perhaps use the prayer of BRF Ministries on page 6. Then read the Bible passage slowly (try reading it aloud if you find it over-familiar), followed by the comment. You can also use *New Daylight* for group study and discussion, if you prefer.

The prayer or point for reflection can be a starting point for your own meditation and prayer. Many people like to keep a journal to record their thoughts about a Bible passage and items for prayer. In *New Daylight* we also note the Sundays and some special festivals from the church calendar, to keep in step with the Christian year.

New Daylight and the Bible

New Daylight contributors use a range of Bible versions, and you will find a list of the versions used opposite. You are welcome to use your own preferred version alongside the passage printed in the notes. This can be particularly helpful if the Bible text has been abridged.

New Daylight affirms that the whole of the Bible is God's revelation to us, and we should read, reflect on and learn from every part of both Old and New Testaments. Usually the printed comment presents a straightforward 'thought for the day', but sometimes it may also raise questions rather than simply providing answers, as we wrestle with some of the more difficult passages of scripture.

New Daylight is also available in a compact size edition. Visit your local Christian bookshop or BRF's online shop **brfonline.org.uk**. To obtain an audio version for the blind or partially sighted, contact Torch Trust for the Blind, Torch House, Torch Way, Northampton Road, Market Harborough LE16 9HL; +44 (0)1858 438260; **info@torchtrust.org**.

Comment on *New Daylight*

To send feedback, please email **enquiries@brf.org.uk**, phone **+44 (0)1865 319700** or write to the address shown opposite.

Writers in this issue

Amy Boucher Pye is a London-based writer, speaker and spiritual director. She has written six books, including *Transforming Love* (Form, 2023) and *Holding onto Hope* (BRF, 2023). Find her at **amyboucherpye.com**.

Tim Heaton is rural dean of Blackmore Vale in the diocese of Salisbury and a non-residentiary canon of Salisbury Cathedral. He is the author of the best-selling Lent course *The Long Road to Heaven* (Circle Books, 2013). You can connect with him at **facebook.com/lentcourses**.

Tony Horsfall is an author, retreat leader and mentor. Among his many books published with BRF are *Knowing You, Jesus*, *Working from a Place of Rest*, *Rhythms of Grace* and *Grief Notes*.

Andy John is Archbishop of Wales. His main interests include sports of most kinds and walking in the hills of north Wales, although he occasionally indulges his terrible taste in music on a rickety old electric guitar.

Ross Moughtin is a retired vicar in the Liverpool diocese. A weekly blogger, he is an active member of his local parkrun.

Elizabeth Rundle is a Methodist Minister living in Dorset. She has led church weekends and quiet days, broadcast on local television and radio. *20 Questions Jesus Asked* (for BRF Ministries) is among her many published Bible studies and devotional books.

Amy Scott Robinson is the author of several books, including *Image of the Invisible* and *Images of Grace* (both for BRF Ministries). She is a regular contributor to *Church Times* and is commissioning editor for children's and youth at Kevin Mayhew.

Sheila Walker is a former associate priest with three rural churches, and has been a teacher, editor, careers adviser, information officer, librarian and writer.

Sally Welch is diocesan canon of Christ Church Cathedral, Oxford and co-director of the Centre for Christian Pilgrimage. She is the former editor of *New Daylight*.

The notes on **artificial intelligence** are written by different people; more details can be found in the 'Meet the authors' section on page 148.

Gordon Giles writes…

It is said that 'time and tide wait for no man'. We find an older version of the phrase in the *Canterbury Tales*, which date from about 1395: 'For thogh we slepe, or wake, or rome, or ryde, Ay fleeth the tyme; it nyl no man abyde.' A tide is not a set of waves upon the seashore, but rather refers to time and the seasons. Chaucer's phrase is not a maritime one, although it has been adopted in common usage, because tides, while not governed by time, do mark time with some regularity. For many the phrase is about ageing: time (tide) does not wait for anyone; we cannot control it or ignore it.

So another year begins, a new tide sweeps in, and with it a new edition of *New Daylight*. A new set of readings brings a blend of the familiar with the new – fresh words and reflections from our authors, aligned to a rhythm of tides which wash upon us with a reliable regularity.

Easter is different every year, but there are rules to determine its date. Easter Day is the first Sunday after the first full moon after the vernal equinox (March 21). Last year Easter was early (March 31), this year much later (April 20). Each Lent and Easter lands with us differently, because a year has turned, in which things have happened, friends and family have been born or died. The sanctuary of our souls has been touched by events, emotions, experiences. This is how God deals with and in us, making fresh what is stale, renewing what is careworn by the tides of time.

The Scottish poet Charles Sorley, who was killed in action in October 1915, aged 20, wrote a poem called 'Expectans Expectavi', inspired by Psalm 40. It serves us well as we stand at the gate of another year:

> *This sanctuary of my soul,*
> *Unwitting I keep white and whole,*
> *Unlatched and lit, if Thou should'st care*
> *To enter or to tarry there.*

> *With parted lips and outstretch'd hands,*
> *And listening ears Thy servant stands.*
> *Call Thou early, call Thou late,*
> *to Thy great service dedicate.*

GORDON GILES

The prayer of BRF Ministries

Faithful God,
thank you for growing BRF Ministries
from small beginnings
into the worldwide family it is today.
We rejoice as young and old
discover you through your word
and grow daily in faith and love.
Keep us humble in your service,
ambitious for your glory
and open to new opportunities.
For your name's sake,
Amen.

'It is such a joy to be part of this amazing project'

As part of our Living Faith ministry, we're raising funds to give away copies of Bible reading notes and other resources to those who aren't able to access them any other way, working with food banks and chaplaincy services, in prisons, hospitals and care homes.

'This very generous gift will be hugely appreciated, and truly bless each recipient… Bless you for your kindness.'

'We would like to send our enormous thanks to all involved. Your generosity will have a significant impact and will help us to continue to provide support to local people in crisis, and for this we cannot thank you enough.'

If you've enjoyed and benefited from our resources, would you consider paying it forward to enable others to do so too?

Make a gift at **brf.org.uk/donate**

Resolutions

One of our family's favourite series of books is about William Brown, the eternal eleven-year-old, whose adventures are documented with exuberance by Richmal Crompton. There is a particular story which always comes to mind at new year, entitled appropriately enough 'William's New Year's Day' from the book of the same title, published in 1922. In this chapter, William is encouraged by Mr Moss, the owner of the local sweet shop, to make a new year's resolution. Having decided that 'bein' perlite' is a most appropriate ambition, William encounters all the challenges that anyone faces who chooses to engage with the new year by embarking on such a project as making a resolution. His practice of adding 'if you don't mind me sayin' so' after the most scurrilous invective mocks all that is wrong about worldly resolutions, while his genuine struggles to remain polite in the face of rudeness is something with which we can all sympathise.

The book is, of course, secular and very much of its time, but the feelings and actions of Mr Moss and William as they struggle through the day are, I suspect, universal. Frivolous though their resolutions are, the lessons learnt can be applied to our own situations, adding a touch of the almost contemporary to the biblical examples which we can also find.

New year's resolutions are often mocked, and equally often taken up only to be swiftly disregarded – apparently the failure rate by mid-February is 80%! But the new year can be a good and productive time, offering as it does an opportunity for prayerful reflection. We can turn our backs on the failures and disappointments of the year gone past and give thanks for all that has brought love, hope and joy into our lives. We can build on all that has been good, rejoicing in our triumphs and taking forward the lessons learnt from our disasters, so that they might not be repeated and so that good fruit might come from them. We can assess our shortcomings, the gaps in our knowledge and our relationships with God and neighbour, and resolve, if not to fill them, at least to make an attempt to do so.

So I wish you a Happy New Year and I encourage you to make some resolutions, praying also for the grace to keep them.

SALLY WELCH

A covenant with ourselves and God

'And now, you priests, this warning is for you… And you will know that I have sent you this warning so that my covenant with Levi may continue,' says the Lord Almighty. 'My covenant was with him, a covenant of life and peace, and I gave them to him; this called for reverence and he revered me and stood in awe of my name. True instruction was in his mouth and nothing false was found on his lips. He walked with me in peace and uprightness, and turned many from sin.'

Young Master Brown's engagement with 'resolutions' begins with the owner of the sweet shop insisting that he must make some: 'Same as giving up sugar in tea in Lent and wearing blue on Oxford and Cambridge Boat Race Day.' William struggles with the suggestions offered to him, as they all seem too difficult. He finally settles on 'being perlite' – 'please and thank you and if you don't mind me sayin' so', and the story relates the challenges involved in keeping this resolution.

Our own resolutions could be similarly shallow – practising courtesy is an excellent thing to do, but hardly life-changing. If we seek true soul growth, perhaps even transformation, we should have ambitions that go deeper than merely polishing our social interactions. Our resolutions could indeed be called 'covenants' – agreements between ourselves and God that we strive to adhere to in the face of opposition from our sinful selves, which tempt us to inertia and apathy at the least, active wrongdoing in the worst case.

God's instructions, relayed through the prophet Malachi, remind us of the original covenant of 'life and peace', and show us that by seeking always to walk with him 'in peace and uprightness', this covenant can be honoured. How to live in peace and uprightness then becomes the question, which is fortunately answered for us countless times in biblical examples, in the lives of the saints and in the examples from our own lives of people whose words and actions align themselves to Christ, as they live out what it means to love God and neighbour.

'And what does the Lord require of you? To act justly and to love mercy and to walk humbly with your God' (Micah 6:8).

SALLY WELCH

Resolving the right thing

As they set out, Jehoshaphat stood and said, 'Listen to me, Judah and people of Jerusalem! Have faith in the Lord your God and you will be upheld; have faith in his prophets and you will be successful.' After consulting the people, Jehoshaphat appointed men to sing to the Lord and to praise him for the splendour of his holiness as they went out at the head of the army, saying: 'Give thanks to the Lord, for his love endures forever.' As they began to sing and praise, the Lord set ambushes against the men of Ammon and Moab and Mount Seir who were invading Judah, and they were defeated.

In recent years the practice of 'manifesting' has become a phenomenon in our society. Simply put, the 'law of attraction' states that 'if you ask the universe for something and genuinely believe you have it already, the universe eventually fulfils your request' (**betterup.com/blog/things-to-manifest**). All that is necessary is to think of something you want, visualise it in detail, ask the universe for it, then 'let go and trust the process'. What a dangerous and corrupt version of prayer this is – worse because it bears some surface similarities with prayer and yet in truth is very far from it indeed.

The people of Israel are not 'manifesting' here – they are not singing praises to God because they have imagined a good outcome and are expecting the stars and planets to align to produce the desired victory. Led by Jehoshaphat, they have spent time in prayer and praise, listening for God's word, obeying his commandments. They are obedient to God's will and in tune with his purposes for them. They are praising God because they trust in him and are certain that any outcome will be his will.

As we make our resolutions for our spiritual journey this year, let us first ensure that we have spent time in prayer and Bible study, listening for his word and aligning ourselves to his will, rather than expecting God to align himself to ours!

'He who did not spare his own Son, but gave him up for us all – how will he not also, along with him, graciously give us all things?' (Romans 8:32).

SALLY WELCH

Making wise resolutions

When Jesus heard this, he said to him, 'You still lack one thing. Sell everything you have and give to the poor, and you will have treasure in heaven. Then come, follow me.' When he heard this, he became very sad, because he was very wealthy. Jesus looked at him and said, 'How hard it is for the rich to enter the kingdom of God! Indeed, it is easier for a camel to go through the eye of a needle than for someone who is rich to enter the kingdom of God.'

What an interesting character this 'ruler' is! We do not know anything more about him than that he obviously has some power and a considerable amount of wealth. But he has heard the words of Jesus and his imagination has been captured by the pictures he has drawn of the kingdom of God. He is a law-abiding, deep-thinking man, who has lived righteously in the eyes of the law all his life. He is, it would seem, fully resolved to do all that is necessary to inherit this 'eternal life' of which Jesus speaks.

But he cannot make that final step; he cannot do all that is being asked of him because his heart and mind are too firmly fixed in the realms of earth rather than the kingdom of heaven. Jesus must have looked at him with such sorrow and love; his response is tender and reflective rather than angry and judgemental. But although he acknowledges the struggles of the man, he will do nothing to help him. It is up to the rich young ruler to make his own choices and determine the future direction of his life.

Our resolutions might be influenced by the world around us, by the people we love, by what we read in the Bible or study in spiritual texts, by our inner convictions or outer circumstances. But they are ours alone. We may indeed ask Christ for help to keep them, but they are ultimately our responsibility.

Heavenly Father, give me the wisdom to make the right choices in my life, the courage and strength to maintain the right path, the determination to set aside all that distracts me from my goal, and the hope of the prize of eternal life which lies ahead.

SALLY WELCH

Resolutions resulting in action

When Jesus reached the spot, he looked up and said to him, 'Zacchaeus, come down immediately. I must stay at your house today.' So he came down at once and welcomed him gladly. All the people saw this and began to mutter, 'He has gone to be the guest of a sinner.' But Zacchaeus stood up and said to the Lord, 'Look, Lord! Here and now I give half of my possessions to the poor, and if I have cheated anybody out of anything, I will pay back four times the amount.'

Mr Moss, the owner of William Brown's local sweet shop, has made the same new year's resolution for ten years – to ask his sweetheart to marry him. William is of the opinion that, given such a record of failure, he should ask someone else, but Mr Moss is determined and his eventual success fills him with joy.

Mr Moss' resolution changes his whole way of life – a good resolution should do that. But it takes more than simply thinking about making a resolution; action is required. When Jesus comes to stay as a guest with Zacchaeus, a tax collector renowned for his cheating ways, there was always the possibility that he would simply arrive, have a good conversation, share a meal and then depart, with nothing significant having changed. Jesus' point about everyone being acceptable in the sight of God would still have been made, in a similar way to that described in Matthew, Mark and Luke, when Jesus eats with 'tax collectors and sinners'.

What makes the story of Zacchaeus stand out is that Zacchaeus' entire life is shown to have been changed. He gives half his wealth to the poor and pays back all those he cheated, even before Jesus arrives at his house to receive his hospitality.

As we reflect on the resolutions we have made, let us ask God for the grace to ensure that we will grow more Christlike as we practise what we know to be right. May our way of life be transformed by our increasing awareness of God's presence, and may what is happening to our souls be reflected in our daily lives.

'You see that a person is considered righteous by what they do and not by faith alone' (James 2:24).

SALLY WELCH

Sacrificial living

'Look,' said Naomi, 'your sister-in-law is going back to her people and her gods. Go back with her.' But Ruth replied, 'Don't urge me to leave you or to turn back from you. Where you go I will go, and where you stay I will stay. Your people will be my people and your God my God. Where you die I will die, and there I will be buried. May the Lord deal with me, be it ever so severely, if even death separates you and me.' When Naomi realised that Ruth was determined to go with her, she stopped urging her.

Dear, brave Ruth! How much courage does it take to turn one's back on all that is safe and easy, comfortable and familiar, and step boldly into an unknown future! 'Where you go, I will go,' she declares, and in those half-dozen words commits herself to the lifelong task of caring for somebody else. With the benefit of hindsight, we can see the happiness that this decision will give, but at her moment of resolution, Ruth can only see the things she is leaving behind – her homeland, her household gods, the chance of another husband from her own tribe, and the new family and new home this will bring her. She turns away from all these and pledges herself to all that this strange God of Naomi might hold for her.

Such quiet heroism, silent sacrificial living, is happening all around us. We might not notice the old man tenderly holding the hand of his confused wife, guiding her without her being aware of it. We might not realise the patience of the mother, weary almost to death, as she rocks her baby to sleep. We might turn over the television channel when news reaches us about the work of peacemakers in conflict-ridden parts of the world or sigh guiltily as we read of those who tend to the sick and the dying, accompanying them on their final journey. Let us make time now, this minute, to thank God for all those who make courageous and selfless decisions and, having made them, have the resolve to keep them.

'Be on your guard; stand firm in the faith; be courageous; be strong'
(1 Corinthians 16:13).

SALLY WELCH

Standing firm

Shadrach, Meshach and Abednego replied to him, 'King Nebuchadnezzar, we do not need to defend ourselves before you in this matter. If we are thrown into the blazing furnace, the God we serve is able to deliver us from it, and he will deliver us from Your Majesty's hand. But even if he does not, we want you to know, Your Majesty, that we will not serve your gods or worship the image of gold you have set up.'

The dramatic action of this story stands out, even amid the general drama of the book of Daniel. Those three devout men, whose names roll gloriously from the tongue, stand firm in front of King Nebuchadnezzar, who under the corrupt guidance of his advisors is demanding that the trio worship a gold idol. The story ends triumphantly – the young men are thrown into the super-heated furnace but do not burn, and Nebuchadnezzar pronounces that no one must speak a word against their god 'for no other god can save in this way' (Daniel 3:29).

What is most thought-provoking, however, is not the saving action in the fiery depths of one who 'looks like a son of the gods' (v. 25). It is the way in which the three young men have resolved not to give way, whatever the cost. More than this, it is the equanimity with which they face the thought of the possible denouement of the action. Whatever the outcome, these men will stand firm and it is with that determination that they enter the fire – without argument or negotiation, prepared either to be rescued or to be burnt alive but absolutely refusing to serve other gods.

The story boy William decides that keeping new year's resolutions is too hard even to maintain for a day: 'I think I've had enough of that bein' p'lite. Will one mornin' do for this year, d'you think?' How firm do we stand when our faith is being challenged – either verbally by colleagues or friends or more indirectly when we are asked to do things which are unjust or unkind? What actions might we take to build up our strength so that we are ready for such challenges?

Lord, let me stand firm so that I might win life (Luke 21:19).

SALLY WELCH

The Epiphany   13

Being realistic

Wisdom makes one wise person more powerful than ten rulers in a city…
All this I tested by wisdom and I said, 'I am determined to be wise' – but
this was beyond me. Whatever exists is far off and most profound – who
can discover it? So I turned my mind to understand, to investigate and
to search out wisdom and the scheme of things and to understand the
stupidity of wickedness and the madness of folly.

'I am determined to be wise' – an excellent ambition, a capital resolution. This, surely is the way to begin the new year, with a statement of grand intent! But then reality kicks in and with admirable honesty, the writer confesses that 'this was beyond me' (v. 23). Instead, he turns his mind to more achievable things, breaking down his goal of wisdom into smaller, more manageable steps. The writer now seeks only to 'understand' wisdom, to investigate it and search it out. I suspect that if he kept to these targets, he would find he had, after a while, achieved his larger ambition.

Very often our failure to keep our resolutions, whether or not they are made on New Year's Day, is caused by our choice of resolution – not because they are inappropriate but because they are far too ambitious and grandiose. That is not to say they are necessarily unachievable, just that setting a huge goal can be self-defeating. Our progress might be very slow, our setbacks many. Better perhaps to have at the back of our minds an end point (wisdom), but in between a number of smaller, manageable steps. Each of these can in turn be broken down into even smaller, bite-size targets. The sense of achievement we get from reaching these mini targets can be a very powerful encouragement as we journey on to our greater goal.

Small changes to our habits are easier to absorb, can more quickly become part of our everyday lives and can in turn be built upon until greater change occurs. And always we have the confidence that, in Christ, lives can be transformed, characters changed, the kingdom brought nearer.

'May these words of my mouth and this meditation of my heart be pleasing
in your sight, Lord, my Rock and my Redeemer' (Psalm 19:14).

SALLY WELCH

Looking forward

I want to know Christ – yes, to know the power of his resurrection and participation in his sufferings, becoming like him in his death, and so, somehow, attaining to the resurrection from the dead. Not that I have already obtained all this, or have already arrived at my goal, but I press on to take hold of that for which Christ Jesus took hold of me. Brothers and sisters, I do not consider myself yet to have taken hold of it. But one thing I do: forgetting what is behind and straining towards what is ahead, I press on towards the goal to win the prize for which God has called me heavenwards in Christ Jesus.

However carefully we make our resolutions, however diligently we work out the steps to our goal, taking care that they should be neither too taxing nor so easy that no progress is made, there is a good chance that we will, at some stage, fail. This failure can take many forms, depending on the sort of resolutions we have made – from sleeping in late and missing out early-morning prayer and Bible study to an angry, hurtful word; from not keeping a commitment to missing an opportunity to offer service to another.

Guilt at our failure is only useful if it spurs us on to greater efforts – it is no use at all if it merely drives us into an apathy in which we even stop trying to attain our goals. Better far to emulate Paul and 'forget what is behind' than wallow in self-pity or self-loathing at our inability to stick to our goals. This is not to deny that failure can have its uses – we can learn where our weak points are, we can try to avoid our 'trigger' moments, those times when we are apt to lapse from our state of effort and give in to temptation. But always we must 'press on', for the prize that awaits us is truly worth the effort.

Lord God, help me to take failure in my stride, to learn its lessons, gather my courage and step out once again towards the goal which you have set for me, in the strength of Christ.

SALLY WELCH

Keeping positive

And so it was with me, brothers and sisters. When I came to you, I did not come with eloquence or human wisdom as I proclaimed to you the testimony about God. For I resolved to know nothing while I was with you except Jesus Christ and him crucified. I came to you in weakness with great fear and trembling. My message and my preaching were not with wise and persuasive words, but with a demonstration of the Spirit's power, so that your faith might not rest on human wisdom, but on God's power.

On January 1, I duly announced at the family breakfast table all the resolutions I had taken for the year. They were a mixture of character formation ('I will be more patient, I will cultivate optimism'), lifestyle ('I will cook more healthy meals') and spiritual ('I will be more intentional in my prayer life'). At the end of this, admittedly lengthy, list my older son wearily announced that the family knew perfectly well already what my resolutions were going to be, as they were the same every year! This caused me some despondency – every year I try so hard; why is it I seem to make so little progress?

But this passage from Paul's letter to the Corinthians gave me hope, and it continues to do so. Yes, I will continue to make resolutions and, yes, I will fail every year – I am human, and failure is built in to us all. But with failure comes humility, with failure comes determination to try again, with failure comes a reliance not on our own strength but on God's, not on our own wisdom, but the power of the Spirit.

'Success is stumbling from failure to failure with no loss of enthusiasm', as Winston Churchill reportedly said, and I like the sound of that. Success is not the opposite of failure, perhaps, but more the result of accepting it, embracing it, recognising our frailties, and then turning to God and leaning on him, so that through us a greater truth might become known and the blazing 'success' of the 'failure' of the crucifixion shines throughout the world.

'My flesh and my heart may fail, but God is the strength of my heart and my portion forever' (Psalm 73:26).

SALLY WELCH

When our resolve is weak

'Watch and pray so that you will not fall into temptation. The spirit is willing, but the flesh is weak'… When he came back, he again found them sleeping, because their eyes were heavy. So he left them and went away once more and prayed the third time, saying the same thing. Then he returned to the disciples and said to them, 'Are you still sleeping and resting? Look, the hour has come, and the Son of Man is delivered into the hands of sinners. Rise! Let us go! Here comes my betrayer!'

On the night before his death, Jesus has led some of his disciples to the Garden of Gethsemane. He begs them to watch and pray with him, but they cannot do even this one simple task which is asked of them. They fall asleep and Jesus is left to suffer his agony unsupported by their prayers and intercessions. This desperate, poignant moment is just the beginning of a series of abandonments and betrayals of Jesus by the people who supposedly loved him dearly and were closest to him. It signals failure on a cosmic scale which affects all who witnessed Christ's final hours.

And yet the risen Christ appears to the same disciples who fled in terror. He calls Peter, whose bravado was shown to be just talk when fear for his own life led him to deny Christ three times, to become the 'rock' on which the church will be founded. He forgives, heals, supports, encourages, while all around him flounder in self-pity, anger, jealousy and fear. He continues to do so, to each one of us, every day, each time we face up to our failures and ask his forgiveness, pledging ourselves once more to walk in the paths of justice and truth, working to bring the kingdom of heaven closer, aligning ourselves as closely as we can with the life of Christ. We know we will not succeed, but we know that sometimes success lies in the attempt and that there is always another day.

Risen Christ, whose glory fills the heavens, whose love suffuses every atom of the universe, whose sacrifice opens the door to eternal life to all who seek it, help us to praise you with every fibre of our being. Alleluia. Amen.

SALLY WELCH

The best example

As the time approached for him to be taken up to heaven, Jesus resolutely set out for Jerusalem. And he sent messengers on ahead, who went into a Samaritan village to get things ready for him; but the people there did not welcome him, because he was heading for Jerusalem. When the disciples James and John saw this, they asked, 'Lord, do you want us to call fire down from heaven to destroy them?' But Jesus turned and rebuked them. Then he and his disciples went to another village.

What an amazing image this passage presents – of Jesus deliberately walking towards the place of his arrest and execution, fully aware of the consequences of this decision, completely determined not to turn away or ignore his task, terrible though it is. How sad that even as he prepares to sacrifice himself for the good of humankind, he is rejected by those same people.

The Samaritan villagers who do not welcome him are not merely being impolite – according to the custom of the time hospitality was a moral obligation. Feeding and sheltering the stranger was a vital part of the culture, springing as it did from the fact that the alternative could be starvation or death at the hands of bandits or wild animals. Not offering hospitality is not a neutral act, it is a hostile one. The disciples would like to punish that village as Elijah did, raining fire upon those who worshipped Baal-Zebub (2 Kings 1). But Jesus will not do this; he simply walks away and continues on his course.

In our resolve to follow lives which copy that of Christ, in our attempts to love God and our neighbour, we may well encounter not just indifference but active hostility. Then it will be our task to remain focused on our goals, to forgive those who would mock or wound us and to continue to work to bring God's kingdom near.

William Brown ends his new year's resolutions at lunch time: 'I think I've had enough of that bein' p'lite.' I wish you well with yours – may they last until next year.

'Because the Sovereign Lord helps me, I will not be disgraced.
Therefore have I set my face like flint, and I know I will not be put to shame.
He who vindicates me is near' (Isaiah 50:7–8a).

SALLY WELCH

If you've enjoyed this set of reflections by **Sally Welch**,
check out her books published with BRF Ministries, including…

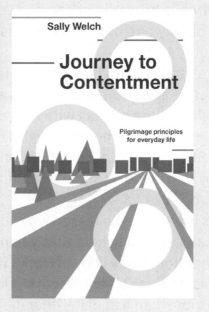

Sharing the Easter Story
From reading to living the gospel

Journey to Contentment
Pilgrimage principles for everyday life

978 1 80039 098 0
£8.99

978 0 85746 592 4
£8.99

To order, visit **brfonline.org.uk** or use the order form at the end.

Living Faith

Luke 10—12

 Among the companions and co-workers of the apostle Paul was a certain Luke, 'the beloved physician' (Colossians 4:14, NRSV). As we know from the Acts of the Apostles, which Luke also wrote, he accompanied Paul on some of his missionary journeys. He may well have given medical assistance to Paul while he was in prison and was with him right to the end. In what was probably one of his final letters, Paul writes: 'Only Luke is with me' (2 Timothy 4:11).

Luke's travels with Paul gave him ample opportunity to gain first-hand knowledge about the life of Jesus and the emerging Christian church. Through his close contact with Paul and other Christian leaders, including those in Jerusalem, he could rightly claim 'to compile a narrative about the events that have been fulfilled among us, just as they were handed on to us by those who from the beginning were eyewitnesses and servants of the word' (Luke 1:1–2).

This is perhaps the reason why Luke's gospel contains so much unique material. It is widely held that when Matthew and Luke wrote their gospels, they both had a copy of Mark's in front of them. The difference is that whereas Matthew takes most of Mark's gospel into his own, Luke uses only a little more than half of it. Other material that is unique to Luke accounts for a full half of his completed gospel. It includes many of the best-loved stories in the Bible, including the shepherds and angels at Bethlehem and the two disciples on the road to Emmaus.

In the three chapters we shall be looking at over the next two weeks, we find a number of these passages that derive from Luke's own sources and appear nowhere else in the New Testament: the return of the 70, the parable of the good Samaritan, Martha distracted by her many tasks, the parable of the friend at midnight and the parable of the rich fool.

Our section comes in the middle of the gospel. Jesus has 'set his face to go to Jerusalem' (9:51) and the plot is driven by the divine necessity of his mission. God's will is at work in human history, but always in contention with human and demonic powers that stand against it.

TIM HEATON

Send reinforcements

After this the Lord appointed seventy others and sent them on ahead of him in pairs to every town and place where he himself intended to go. He said to them, 'The harvest is plentiful, but the labourers are few; therefore ask the Lord of the harvest to send out labourers into his harvest. Go on your way… Whenever you enter a town and its people welcome you, eat what is set before you; cure the sick who are there, and say to them, "The kingdom of God has come near to you."'

Although only Luke reports the mission of the 70, much of what we find here repeats the instructions given to the twelve in Mark and Matthew, as well as earlier in Luke (9:1–6). It is, therefore, a reprise of the mission of the twelve, the larger group of followers conveying a sense of growth and progress. The significance of the number 70 can probably be traced to the list of nations in Genesis 10, so that the mission of the 70 predicts the eventual mission of the church to the whole world.

Jesus' followers are charged with continuing the three facets of his own work: creating community (table fellowship), healing the sick and proclaiming the kingdom. As with the twelve, God chooses to act by involving human workers as his agents. The 70 are instructed to pray for 'the Lord of the harvest to send out labourers into his harvest' (v. 2), which turns out to be them. They are the labourers; the response to their prayer is their own mission to the needy people of God. Remember that you, too, can be the answer to your own prayers, so be careful what you pray for!

That is the key point here, I think: God works through people. Not only through miracles and divine mysteries and his holy angels, but also through people. It sounds obvious to us now, I know, but this is where the Christian mission began, first with the twelve and then with the 70. This is our commissioning, too; this is our authority to act in Jesus' name.

Lord of the harvest, make me an instrument of your mission to the world and use me to further the work of your kingdom. Amen.

TIM HEATON

Mission accomplished

The seventy returned with joy, saying, 'Lord, in your name even the demons submit to us!' He said to them, 'I watched Satan fall from heaven like a flash of lightning. See, I have given you authority to tread on snakes and scorpions, and over all the power of the enemy; and nothing will hurt you. Nevertheless, do not rejoice at this, that the spirits submit to you, but rejoice that your names are written in heaven.'

Every mission, military or otherwise, must result in success or failure, or perhaps some partial achievement of the goal. The objective in this case seems to have been fully accomplished, and the return of the 70 is characterised by 'joy' (v. 17). There is joyfulness in what God is doing in the work of the disciples, and their success is epitomised in their power over demons. Acting in Jesus' name (v. 17) and with his authority (v. 19) enables the disciples to perform mighty deeds.

Snakes and scorpions appear as images for the power of evil. Jesus' authority to tread on them is not to be taken literally, so please do not try this at home, brothers and sisters; I cannot assure you of divine protection! The language here is figurative, not literal. The Bible is full of such imagery for Satan, not least the serpent in Genesis 3, and by casting out demons the disciples have demonstrated their power over evil; they have metaphorically trodden on snakes and scorpions.

The work of the disciples has even greater significance than they may have appreciated. We know that the end times will be marked by a conflict between God and Satan, in which Satan will be defeated (Revelation 12:7–9), so their success signals the coming of God's reign on earth. Their power to liberate others from demons is a sign that the promise of the end times is being realised now.

Yet there is an even greater reason for rejoicing: the disciples' names have been 'written in heaven' (v. 20), in the book of life, as has yours and the names of all who serve the Lord.

Empowering God, may joy always be my response to the defeat of evil, the dawning of your kingdom and the heaven that awaits me. Amen.

TIM HEATON

The good neighbour

Jesus replied, 'A man was going down from Jerusalem to Jericho and fell into the hands of robbers, who stripped him, beat him, and took off, leaving him half dead. Now by chance a priest was going down that road, and when he saw him he passed by on the other side. So likewise a Levite, when he came to the place and saw him, passed by on the other side. But a Samaritan while travelling came upon him, and when he saw him he was moved with compassion. He went to him and bandaged his wounds... Which of these three, do you think, was a neighbour to the man who fell into the hands of the robbers?' He said, 'The one who showed him mercy.'

The parable of the good Samaritan follows an exchange with a clever lawyer (a teacher of the law) who asked Jesus what he must do to inherit eternal life. In reply, Jesus quotes the twin commandments to love God (Deuteronomy 6:5) and to love one's neighbour (Leviticus 19:18). But the lawyer is not satisfied and asks: 'And who is my neighbour?' (Luke 10:29).

To fully appreciate the parable, it is important to understand the feud that had existed for centuries between Judea and Samaria. Samaritans were a remnant of the northern kingdom of Israel; they had intermarried with their Assyrian conquerors and their Judaic faith had absorbed elements of pagan religion. To their Jewish neighbours they were unclean – foreigners, outsiders and enemies. So, in a dramatic and unexpected twist to the tale, your neighbour turns out to be someone you even think of as your enemy.

The parable demolishes all boundaries and divisions when it comes to defining 'neighbour'. Social position, race, religion and nationality count for nothing. Moreover, the definition of neighbour is changed from one who *receives* kindness to one who *bestows* kindness. Neighbours are defined actively not passively. Many countries in the world today have a 'good Samaritan law', making it a requirement for citizens to assist a person in danger or, at the very least, call for help, and not pass by on the other side.

Merciful Father, may I show my love for you by showing compassion to others, regardless of who they are or who I think I am. Amen.

TIM HEATON

Devotion to God's word

Now as they went on their way, he entered a certain village where a woman named Martha welcomed him. She had a sister named Mary, who sat at Jesus' feet and listened to what he was saying. But Martha was distracted by her many tasks, so she came to him and asked, 'Lord, do you not care that my sister has left me to do all the work by myself? Tell her, then, to help me.' But the Lord answered her, 'Martha, Martha, you are worried and distracted by many things, but few things are needed – indeed only one. Mary has chosen the better part, which will not be taken away from her.'

Jesus adheres to the travelling instructions he previously gave to his disciples: whenever you enter a town and its people welcome you, eat what is set before you (Luke 10:8). Accordingly, in an unnamed village, Martha welcomes Jesus and begins to prepare a meal for him. Mary sits at his feet. We can see nothing wrong with that by our customs today, but it was a radical violation of the social rules of the time.

Jesus supports Mary and says what she has chosen – the better alternative – 'will not be taken away from her' (v. 42). It is a reminder of the overriding importance of devotion to God's word as an expression of one's love for God. Today, right now, you are showing the same devotion by reading this! Martha, who on the face of it had done nothing wrong and was simply fulfilling the conventions of her society, had allowed secondary matters to distract her from the one thing that must take precedence over all other concerns.

The story forms a doublet with the parable of the good Samaritan: Mary loves her Lord; the Samaritan loves his neighbour. Together they are model disciples. Moreover, they are unlikely heroes: a woman and a foreigner. As a composite they represent all marginalised people, and the conjunction of these stories powerfully voices Jesus' protest against the boundaries and divisions set by the culture in which he lived.

God of the outsider, help me to observe the only two rules of your kingdom: to love you and to love my neighbour. Amen.

TIM HEATON

The friend at midnight

Then Jesus said to them, 'Suppose you have a friend, and you go to him at midnight and say, "Friend, lend me three loaves of bread; a friend of mine on a journey has come to me, and I have no food to offer him." And suppose the one inside answers, "Don't bother me. The door is already locked, and my children and I are in bed. I can't get up and give you anything." I tell you, even though he will not get up and give you the bread because of friendship, yet because of your shameless audacity he will surely get up and give you as much as you need.'

The Lord's Prayer in Luke 11:2–4 is followed by this assurance that God will always answer our prayer. To fully appreciate the parable, it is important to understand that hospitality was such a serious duty in first-century Palestine that any failure to provide for a guest would bring shame on the host. The parable invites you to put yourself in the position of someone who has received an unexpected guest but has no food to give him.

With 'shameless audacity' (v. 8) – just 'shamelessness' in the original Greek – you go to your friend in the middle of the night to borrow bread. You are not ashamed to do this; you are prepared to act shamelessly to avoid the worse shame of being a bad host. Will your sleeping friend turn you away? No, such a thing would be unimaginable given the social customs of the time. It would be shameful of your friend if they refused to help you; it would bring disgrace on them. The honour code demands that they assist you, if not out of friendship then at least to preserve their good name.

Accordingly, no other outcome to the story is conceivable – you will have your bread. The parable, therefore, reaches a straightforward conclusion: if your friend is so certain to answer your plea for help, even at such an unsocial hour, then how much more surely will God answer you when you cry out to him in need.

Faithful God, your goodness to me is greater than that of any friend;
you are more reliable than any neighbour: hear my prayer. Amen.

TIM HEATON

Ruler of demons

Now he was casting out a demon that was mute; when the demon had gone out, the one who had been mute spoke, and the crowds were amazed. But some of them said, 'He casts out demons by Beelzebul, the ruler of the demons.' Others, to test him, kept demanding from him a sign from heaven. But he knew what they were thinking and said to them, 'Every kingdom divided against itself is laid waste, and a divided house-hold falls. If Satan also is divided against himself, how will his kingdom stand? – for you say that I cast out the demons by Beelzebul... But if it is by the finger of God that I cast out the demons, then the kingdom of God has come upon you.'

In the New Testament the word 'demon' is used to mean a spiritual entity hostile to both God and people. Jesus is pictured as being in continual conflict with evil spirits opposed to his work, but the people who contested his ministry tried to link him with these very forces of evil rather than recognising his divine origin. To cast out demons was not easy; it required a power greater than human power, and they attributed Jesus' success to the indwelling of Satan.

Beelzebul was a pagan god whose name had become synonymous with Satan. Jesus' exorcisms represented a direct assault on Satan's power, so to counter the accusation that he casts out demons in the name of Beelzebul Jesus points out that if he were Satan's ally the exorcisms would represent a mutiny. How can Satan cast out Satan?

As we saw on Monday, the success of the 70 in casting out demons signalled the coming of God's reign on earth. Here again, the breaking of Satan's power is evidence that the kingdom of God has come upon them (v. 20). Yet evil still abounds in our world today in many forms and manifestations, like discrimination, exploitation and oppression. It is down to us now, Christ's present-day disciples, to continue the stand against evil and to pray, as we do in the Lord's Prayer, for our deliverance from it.

Loving Father, keep me alert to the enmity of Satan to your kingdom, and help me to name evil powers for what they are. Amen.

TIM HEATON

The sign of Jonah

When the crowds were increasing, he began to say, 'This generation is an evil generation; it asks for a sign, but no sign will be given to it except the sign of Jonah. For just as Jonah became a sign to the people of Nineveh, so the Son of Man will be to this generation… The people of Nineveh will rise up at the judgement with this generation and condemn it, because they repented at the proclamation of Jonah, and indeed, something greater than Jonah is here!'

We saw yesterday how some in the crowds kept demanding from Jesus 'a sign from heaven' (Luke 11:16), even though he had just exorcised a demon and the crowds were amazed! In today's verses we find Jesus responding directly to their request: no sign will be given except the sign of Jonah. We know that Jonah was a Hebrew prophet and the central character of the Old Testament book that bears his name, but what does Jesus mean by the 'sign of Jonah'?

Jonah is best known for spending three days and nights in the belly of a large fish (Jonah 1:17), so it would be quite natural to think that the sign of Jonah points forward to the time when the Son of Man will spend three days and nights in the darkness of the tomb. In fact, that is the very meaning spelled out in Matthew's gospel (Matthew 12:40) – but not so here in Luke. Here the sign is Jonah himself and his prophetic message, a call to repentance.

The people of Nineveh repented as a result of Jonah's message, but this 'evil generation' (v. 29) has not been receptive to Jesus and his proclamation of the kingdom. They have heard someone far greater than Jonah but have not listened. They need no other sign – and no other sign will be given to them – except the sign of Jonah: hear the word of God and do his will, just as the Ninevites did. As we discovered on Wednesday in the story of Martha and Mary, commitment to God's word is paramount. Then the kingdom comes.

God of Jonah, your Son Jesus is greater than any prophet; may his word inform all that I think and say and do, today and always. Amen.

TIM HEATON

The light of life

'No one after lighting a lamp puts it in a cellar or under a bushel basket; rather, one puts it on the lampstand so that those who enter may see the light. Your eye is the lamp of your body. If your eye is healthy, your whole body is full of light, but if it is unhealthy, your body is full of darkness. Therefore consider whether the light in you is not darkness. But if your whole body is full of light, with no part of it in darkness, it will be as full of light as when a lamp gives you light with its rays.'

Light is a recurring biblical motif and a powerful symbol of the new life we have in Christ, especially in these dark winter months. Advent is a journey from darkness to light, leading us to Christmas when the light that we long for finally comes into the world. Jesus is the light of the world (John 8:12), and his divine radiance shines in us so that we, too, may be lights in the world (Matthew 5:14–16).

Here Luke picks up the theme. We know from modern medicine that light enters the eye to give sight, but in ancient times the eye was thought to emit light from inside the body so that objects could be seen. Accordingly, the eye is 'the lamp of the body' (v. 34), releasing light from within the disciple. In a similar way, the eye is the window of the soul ('These lovely lamps, these windows of the soul' – Guillaume de Salluste Du Bartas, 1544–90), communicating to others something of our innermost thoughts and how we are feeling inside.

The light that Jesus gives should fill the whole person, but it does not because 'this generation is an evil generation' (11:29). They cannot see Jesus because the light within them has turned to darkness. It concludes a long and hostile confrontation that began with the exorcism of the demon, which as a single piece sharpens the question of where God's power is at work. The answer, of course, is in Jesus, and through him in us.

Father of lights, in you there is no darkness at all; may the bright beam of your presence shine in my heart to bring light to others. Amen.

TIM HEATON

Purity and false piety

While he was speaking, a Pharisee invited him to dine with him, so he went in and took his place at the table. The Pharisee was amazed to see that he did not first wash before dinner. Then the Lord said to him, 'Now you Pharisees clean the outside of the cup and of the dish, but inside you are full of greed and wickedness. You fools! Did not the one who made the outside make the inside also? So give as alms those things that are within and then everything will be clean for you.'

The stage is set for another confrontation when Jesus takes his place at the table of a Pharisee without having washed first. The Pharisees observed strict rules about ritual cleanliness, which had far more to do with obedience to the law of Moses than with hygiene. By not washing, especially after having just performed an exorcism and been in contact with the crowds, Jesus shocks his host.

But Jesus is less concerned with rites of purity than with the purity of one's heart. A person's actions should reflect their inner cleanness, and Jesus accuses the Pharisees of being 'full of greed and wickedness' (v. 39), because they are not generous to the poor. The contrast between outside and inside is a charge of hypocrisy: they clean the outside of their tableware but inside they are not clean. Jesus tells them that if they were to give alms to the poor then they will be as clean on the inside as their crockery is on the outside. Charitable giving is an effective antidote to greed.

The episode is followed by Jesus' pronouncement of the famous 'woes' against the Pharisees and the teachers of the law – declarations of God's judgement. They amount to a searching and uncomfortable indictment of a piety so misdirected that it cloaks greed and wickedness within: searching, because it uncovers a multitude of hypocrisies for which they shall one day face judgement; uncomfortable, because it serves as a warning to us not to fall into the same traps of false piety ourselves.

God of the Pharisees, I know I am not perfect either; keep me from hypocrisy and set my mind on those in need of any kind. Amen.

TIM HEATON

Do not be afraid

'I tell you, my friends, do not fear those who kill the body and after that can do nothing more. But I will show you whom to fear: fear the one who, after killing, has authority to cast into hell. Yes, I tell you, fear that one! Are not five sparrows sold for two pennies? Yet not one of them is forgotten in God's sight. But even the hairs of your head are all numbered. Do not be afraid; you are of more value than many sparrows.'

Jesus has just warned the Pharisees and teachers of the law to be ready for the judgement-to-come, when their false piety and hypocrisy will be revealed. Now he tells his 'friends' (v. 4) they have no need to fear the persecution-to-come. They might be killed, for sure, but their persecutors will then have no further power over them: they cannot be cast into hell. Death, therefore, should not be their ultimate fear; rather they should fear God, who alone has the power to cast into hell. To 'fear' God is used here in the distinctive biblical sense, meaning to honour, respect and obey, rather than 'to be afraid of'.

Lest we should be in any doubt about that, Jesus goes on to assure his disciples that they have no need whatsoever to be afraid of God. In fact, quite the opposite. He gives us one of scripture's most beautiful and endearing assurances of God's care for everyone who does his will. If God does not forget even an individual sparrow, a creature so commonplace and seemingly of such little value (literally two-a-penny), then we should have no doubt at all regarding God's concern for all who follow Jesus.

And let us not leave it there: I believe that God loves every human being, and that the severity of his judgement will be matched measure for measure by the depth of his mercy and forgiveness. God will forget no one. We should be in no uncertainty about the infinite worth of every human life in God's sight – and every sparrow's, too.

God of all creation, you love and care for everything you have made;
strengthen my faith that you are always there for me. Amen.

TIM HEATON

The rich fool

Then he told them a parable: 'The land of a rich man produced abundantly. And he thought to himself, "What should I do, for I have no place to store my crops?" Then he said, "I will do this: I will pull down my barns and build larger ones, and there I will store all my grain and my goods. And I will say to my soul, Soul, you have ample goods laid up for many years; relax, eat, drink, be merry." But God said to him, "You fool! This very night your life is being demanded of you. And the things you have prepared, whose will they be?" So it is with those who store up treasures for themselves but are not rich towards God.'

There is a common, prideful inclination among humankind to think that we can make it on our own, that we do not need anyone else nor do we need God. That was the rich man's folly in a parable that sketches the figure of a man who thinks he is self-sufficient but leaves God out of the reckoning.

He can provide for himself, and his supplies will last him for many years. He needs not the security and love of family, friends, community or God. His self-centredness is reflected in his language: *my* crops, *my* barns, *my* grain, *my* goods, *my* soul. The man has shut out everyone else from his life and thoughts. There is no one else in the story except the man and his possessions – until God exposes the poverty of his abundance.

The thought of what he might be able to do for those in need never enters his mind. If his fields have brought forth abundantly it is a blessing from God, which demands faithfulness in making provision for others, but his thoughts reveal he has no sense of responsibility either to his community or the welfare of people less fortunate than he.

Does the story hold up a mirror before us? Does it expose our innermost thoughts as clearly as it does those of the rich fool?

Generous God, do not let greed eat away at my compassion; help me to take a good look at my life and listen to my own inner voices. Amen.

TIM HEATON

Do not worry

He said to his disciples, 'Therefore I tell you, do not worry about your life, what you will eat, or about your body, what you will wear. For life is more than food and the body more than clothing. Consider the ravens: they neither sow nor reap, they have neither storehouse nor barn, and yet God feeds them. Of how much more value are you than the birds! And which of you by worrying add a single hour to your span of life? If then you are not able to do so small a thing as that, why do you worry about the rest?'

The futility of worrying over food and clothing drives home the lesson of yesterday's parable about the rich fool. Indeed, today's verses follow on directly from that and are linked to the parable by Jesus' opening word 'Therefore'. The rich fool's concern for material goods is now extended to the fundamental human anxiety for basic survival needs: food and clothing. While these are natural and legitimate concerns, Jesus offers three reasons why we should not fret over them.

First, 'life is more than food and the body more than clothing' (v. 23). These words are not intended for those who are starving and have nothing; they are addressed to those of us who have food to eat and clothes to wear yet spend our lives trying to acquire more and forget about the higher things.

Second, like the ravens (and Tuesday's sparrows), we should place our trust more in God's providence. The comment that they have 'neither storehouse nor barn' (v. 24) reminds us that the rich fool's grain stores offered him no security at all.

Third, it is just common sense: being anxious will not solve any of our problems.

Faith in Jesus can set us free from our obsession with material things. Then we may find that some of the things we have been concerned about are really not that significant at all. We may also realise that we have not given enough time to important matters like family, friends and God.

Liberating God, there is more to life than the things I spend my life seeking;
help me to spend more time on things that really matter. Amen.

TIM HEATON

The need for watchfulness

'Be dressed ready for service and keep your lamps burning, like servants waiting for their master to return from a wedding banquet, so that when he comes and knocks they can immediately open the door for him. It will be good for those servants whose master finds them watching when he comes. Truly I tell you, he will dress himself to serve, will have them recline at the table and will come and wait on them. It will be good for those servants whose master finds them ready, even if he comes in the middle of the night or towards daybreak... You also must be ready, because the Son of Man will come at an hour when you do not expect him.'

Our culture is unfamiliar with the conventions that defined the relationship between masters and servants, yet what these verses still give us today is a metaphorical measure of the complete dedication to Jesus and his kingdom which is asked of us. We are being encouraged to be as faithful to Jesus as devoted servants were to their masters.

We are also being urged to be vigilant: 'It will be good for those servants whose master finds them watching when he comes' (v. 37). This is a blessing upon those who are ready, and there is a clear reference here to the expected *parousia*, the second coming of Christ, when all will be judged. The faithful who are ready at the Lord's return will find happiness and joy. In a dramatic reversal of roles, we are told the master will serve the servants at the great banquet in heaven, just as Jesus' earthly ministry was characterised by service: 'I am among you as one who serves' (Luke 22:27).

But what does it mean to be ready? Given what we have encountered in these chapters of the gospel, we might suppose it to mean loving God and loving our neighbour, devoting ourselves to God's word, opposing evil, putting away all hypocrisy, handling our material possessions faithfully, being generous to those in need, trusting in God's providence and serving others.

God our judge, may you find me dressed ready for service and with my lamps burning when you come again in glory. Amen.

TIM HEATON

Decision and division

'I have come to cast fire upon the earth, and how I wish it were already ablaze! I have a baptism with which to be baptised, and what constraint I am under until it is completed! Do you think that I have come to bring peace to the earth? No, I tell you, but rather division! From now on five in one household will be divided, three against two and two against three; they will be divided: father against son and son against father, mother against daughter and daughter against mother, mother-in-law against her daughter-in-law and daughter-in-law against mother-in-law.'

We end this series on a difficult note for those who have experienced division within their own families because of their discipleship of Christ. This is an unhappy situation and one that sadly mirrors the opposition we may encounter in the world at large: wherever the word of God has been heard, division has occurred among the people who heard it. Here Jesus warns that those who make a commitment to him will find their relationships with others affected by that commitment.

Although the kingdom of God is characterised by peace and reconciliation, the announcement of that kingdom is always going to be divisive, because it requires decision and some form of action. Jesus himself was not spared from opposition and rejection, and indeed would become the first casualty of his own proclamation of the gospel: his 'baptism' (v. 50) is probably an allusion to his death, which is now not far away. So, peace will come though not immediately; conflict will precede reconciliation.

We cannot make a commitment to Christ as Lord without it affecting the way we relate to others. This is because, if it is to be any real commitment at all, it will shape our values, priorities, goals and behaviour. It will force us to change our old ways and patterns of life, and these changes may precipitate turning points in our relationships with others, even friends and those closest to us. We who have chosen to follow Jesus must prepare for the opposition we shall face, sometimes even from our own families.

God of peace and concord, I pray for families and relationships riven by faith and unbelief: bring them your reconciling love. Amen.

TIM HEATON

Isaac: promised son

When we think of Isaac, son of Abraham and Sarah, the first picture that comes to mind might be that of a young boy stretched out on a pile of wood, his father ready to sacrifice him. But in researching his life, I learned that some Bible commentators think Isaac could have been even 30 years old then – and thus strong enough to overpower his father. Yet God provided an alternative and saved Abraham from having to obey his command. This story is so well known because it heralds the sacrifice that God the Father made when he sent Jesus to die for our sins to fulfil the requirements of the law.

Now for a few moments, I invite you to imagine yourself as Isaac. You know that you are the answer to decades of prayers and that the hopes of the nation will be fulfilled through you. Although you are the promised child of the chosen people, your life will not be without pain, betrayal or heartache.

Picture yourself meeting your future spouse, chosen by God to be your life partner. Your eyes meet across the fields and love blossoms. You might think the scene will morph into soft focus, music swelling while the credits roll. But the story does not end with that romantic scene. Instead, your family is split after you and your spouse each align yourselves with a son. This will eventually tear your family apart, with both parents bereft of the beloved offspring. Heartache, betrayal and pain, but God never abandons Isaac or his family.

Imagining ourselves as Isaac – over many centuries and through different cultures – is easier than we may have thought because we can relate to his suffering and struggles. We therefore can be encouraged at how God continues to love them, never giving up on them no matter how much they fail him. Although these people wander from God and are wayward, he is constant. Their lives may be messy, but God does not abandon them.

As with them, so too with us. No matter how much we fail God or each other, he waits for us with open arms, welcoming us back home. He will restore us and renew us – we need only to look to him.

AMY BOUCHER PYE

A promise fulfilled

Now the Lord was gracious to Sarah as he had said, and the Lord did for Sarah what he had promised. Sarah became pregnant and bore a son to Abraham in his old age, at the very time God had promised him. Abraham gave the name Isaac to the son Sarah bore him. When his son Isaac was eight days old, Abraham circumcised him, as God commanded him. Abraham was a hundred years old when his son Isaac was born to him. Sarah said, 'God has brought me laughter, and everyone who hears about this will laugh with me.' And she added, 'Who would have said to Abraham that Sarah would nurse children? Yet I have borne him a son in his old age.'

Our journey with Isaac begins with his improbable birth. Born to parents who were 90 and 100, he was an answer to a long-before given promise. The Lord God had said to Abraham and Sarah that they would be parents – through her formerly barren womb and not, as they subsequently arranged, by her servant. Although at times they wavered in their belief, God did not renege on fulfilling what he said he would do. They simply were not party to his timeline and had to keep trusting.

When God affirmed his promise to Abraham that he would become a dad, Abraham laughed with disbelief (see Genesis 17:17). Sarah, when she gave birth to their son, also laughed. How else, she observed, could someone respond to this amazing miracle? They then followed God's command and named him Isaac, which means laughter; this long-desired son brought forth joy and rejoicing to those who previously had been tempted to give up hope.

We can find heartening encouragement from our ancient forbears and how they continued to believe, year after year. When we discern God's promises in our lives, especially those from the Bible, we can hang onto the hope and belief that he will fulfil them, however unlikely it may appear from our perspective.

Loving God, you promise that you will never leave nor forsake me. Help me to believe that what you say is true and applies to me. Amen.

AMY BOUCHER PYE

A severe test

Some time later God tested Abraham. He said to him, 'Abraham!' 'Here I am,' he replied. Then God said, 'Take your son, your only son, whom you love – Isaac – and go to the region of Moriah. Sacrifice him there as a burnt offering on a mountain that I will show you.' Early the next morning Abraham got up and loaded his donkey. He took with him two of his servants and his son Isaac. When he had cut enough wood for the burnt offering, he set out for the place God had told him about. On the third day Abraham looked up and saw the place in the distance. He said to his servants, 'Stay here with the donkey while I and the boy go over there. We will worship and then we will come back to you.'

When the character of Isaac comes to mind, we may think first of this story of God testing Abraham, calling him to sacrifice his son. And our immediate question might be how could the Lord, who condemns child sacrifice, ask such a thing? Theologians cannot give a definitive answer, but in wondering about this conundrum, we can focus on two words from this scripture passage.

The first is *test*. God called Abraham to lead his people, and perhaps he posed this trial as part of his determining if Abraham was ready. Would Abraham obey, or not? How would his chosen leader grow through this test?

The other word is *love*. Note that this is the first time this word appears in scripture. God knows that Abraham loves his son dearly; he thus does not make his request lightly. Love is implied in the story too. Not only that Abraham loves God, because he obeys his command, but that Isaac loves Abraham. After all, Isaac probably was old and strong enough to overpower his father physically.

God may allow us to go through periods of testing, by which he refines us and clarifies our character and actions. But we can trust that his foundation of love will never fail us.

Almighty God, I wonder about the mysteries concerning you.
Please give me wisdom and understanding to grasp who you are
and your love for me. Amen.

AMY BOUCHER PYE

God will provide

Abraham took the wood for the burnt offering and placed it on his son Isaac, and he himself carried the fire and the knife. As the two of them went on together, Isaac spoke up and said to his father Abraham, 'Father?' 'Yes, my son?' Abraham replied. 'The fire and wood are here,' Isaac said, 'but where is the lamb for the burnt offering?' Abraham answered, 'God himself will provide the lamb for the burnt offering, my son.' And the two of them went on together.

Perhaps so many Christians today resonate with this gripping story because of its parallels with the sacrifice that God the Father made by sending his Son Jesus to die on the cross. The main and obvious similarity is a loving father being called to sacrifice his son. Other parallels may be less significant but are compelling, such as God calling Abraham, who lived in a mountainous area, to journey to a different mountain – Mount Moriah. This place carried weight in later centuries; here Solomon built the temple, and many scholars believe that here Jesus carried his cross and died.

Another parallel relates to the wood that would be used to kill the victim. Abraham gave Isaac the wood to carry for the sacrifice, even as Jesus carried his wooden cross. Another is that Abraham and Isaac's journey took three days, and Jesus journeyed from death to life in three days.

But what is so striking in this story is Abraham's strong belief that God will provide. Whatever he felt on the inside, which is not revealed in the narrative, he expressed his faith in God while following God's instructions. As he moved through the motions of finding the location and placing the wood in a pile, perhaps he thought that God would raise Isaac from the dead.

What God asks us will differ from this great test of Abraham, but we can place our wholehearted belief in him and his promises. We can trust that however unlikely it may appear from the outside circumstances, he will provide.

Loving God, when I face excruciating things – in my family, health, work, relationships – help me to turn to you and believe that you will provide what I need. Amen.

AMY BOUCHER PYE

Fearing the Lord

But the angel of the Lord called out to him from heaven, 'Abraham! Abraham!' 'Here I am,' he replied. 'Do not lay a hand on the boy,' he said... 'Now I know that you fear God, because you have not withheld from me your son, your only son.' Abraham looked up and there in a thicket he saw a ram caught by its horns. He... sacrificed it as a burnt offering instead of his son. So Abraham called that place The Lord Will Provide... The angel of the Lord called to Abraham from heaven a second time and said, 'I swear by myself, declares the Lord, that because you have done this and have not withheld your son, your only son, I will surely bless you and make your descendants as numerous as the stars in the sky and as the sand on the seashore.'

Lately I have been considering how fearing the Lord is not valued as much as it was previously. A reviewer of one of my books noted that I speak about God as a friend, instead of as someone I have 'put on a Godly pedestal'. I am grateful for how the reviewer noticed the intimacy in my relationship with God, but I also want to continue to honour and obey God. I would love for a healthy fear of the Lord, which elsewhere in scripture says is the beginning of wisdom (Proverbs 9:10), to shine through me.

The angel of the Lord noted this submissive stance in Abraham; because Abraham followed the Lord's commands, God knew that he honoured and feared him. Interestingly, the angel of the Lord may be an angel or could be the Deity himself (such as Jesus). When the angel calls to Abraham the second time, he speaks as the Lord.

We see the power of Abraham's honouring of God through a summary of the story: God tested Abraham; Abraham feared the Lord; God said he would fulfil his promise to make Abraham a father to many. As you ponder Abraham's faithful response, consider how God might be calling you to fear and honour him today.

Faithful God, help me to hear and obey you. I want to honour you with my thoughts, words and actions. Amen.

AMY BOUCHER PYE

Trusting in God

'I want you to swear by the Lord, the God of heaven and the God of earth, that you will not get a wife for my son from the daughters of the Canaanites, among whom I am living, but will go to my country and my own relatives and get a wife for my son Isaac.' The servant asked him, 'What if the woman is unwilling to come back with me to this land? Shall I then take your son back to the country you came from?' 'Make sure that you do not take my son back there,' Abraham said. 'The Lord, the God of heaven, who brought me out of my father's household and my native land and who spoke to me and promised me on oath, saying, "To your offspring I will give this land" – he will send his angel before you so that you can get a wife for my son from there.'

As Abraham reaches the end of his life, he is keen to ensure that Isaac will receive God's promises to make Abraham the father of many nations. A key part includes Isaac not leaving the promised land – not being tempted away from his inheritance – and not marrying from outside his people group. Thus the biblical narrative details the arrangements Abraham makes with his servant, including the strong oath, to emphasise the importance of God honouring the request.

Again a notable aspect from this story is Abraham's sure belief that God will provide just the right wife for Isaac. He is willing to release his servant from this important quest if God does not come through. Because Abraham believes that God will not fail him, he is assured that the servant will have success.

How often do we believe with such strong faith that God will not fail us? Perhaps today you could look back over the past week or month prayerfully, asking God to show you how he has been with you, leading and guiding. As we remind ourselves of God's faithfulness, we may then find it easier to trust when we face challenges and trials.

God of the impossible, I believe in your promises; help me when I find it hard to believe and trust in you. Amen.

AMY BOUCHER PYE

Success granted

'When I came to the spring today, I said, "Lord, God of my master Abraham, if you will, please grant success to the journey on which I have come. See, I am standing beside this spring. If a young woman comes out to draw water and I say to her, 'Please let me drink a little water from your jar', and if she says to me, 'Drink, and I'll draw water for your camels too', let her be the one the Lord has chosen for my master's son." Before I finished praying in my heart, Rebekah came out, with her jar on her shoulder. She went down to the spring and drew water, and I said to her, "Please give me a drink." She quickly lowered her jar from her shoulder and said, "Drink, and I'll water your camels too." So I drank, and she watered the camels also.'

Sometimes God in his mercy answers our prayers even before we finish uttering them. This is what happened to Abraham's servant. Knowing the importance of his task, he asked for confirmation that this was the right woman for Isaac, specifying in his request that she would water the camels too. And thus she did, going back ten times for water for each camel. He knew that God had honoured not only his prayers but the prayers of his master.

At times when we go to God with heartfelt pleas and burdens he may appear silent, and so reading a story of this instant answer might fill us with painful longing. God might then be refining our faith, or we might be asking for something outside his good purposes. When we experience this kind of 'dark night of the soul', we can continue to move towards God even in the silence as we yearn and seek his comfort, grace and acts of mercy, trusting all the while that he hears us and loves us.

When God delivers his response in a way we would not have anticipated, we can find hope in stories such as this one, when he grants his favour and mercy in a clear manner.

'Then the word of the Lord came to Jeremiah: "I am the Lord, the God of all mankind. Is anything too hard for me?"' (Jeremiah 32:26–27).

AMY BOUCHER PYE

A love match

Then they said, 'Let's call the young woman and ask her about it.' So they called Rebekah and asked her, 'Will you go with this man?' 'I will go,' she said…. [Isaac] went out to the field one evening to meditate, and as he looked up, he saw camels approaching. Rebekah also looked up and saw Isaac. She got down from her camel and asked the servant, 'Who is that man in the field coming to meet us?' 'He is my master,' the servant answered. So she took her veil and covered herself. Then the servant told Isaac all he had done. Isaac brought her into the tent of his mother Sarah, and he married Rebekah. So she became his wife, and he loved her; and Isaac was comforted after his mother's death.

At least at the beginning of their marriage, Isaac and Rebekah appear to enjoy not only an arranged marriage but a love match too. Perhaps part of their joy relates to how the woman's consent is affirmed – when her mother and brother ask her if she is willing to leave her home to marry an unknown man, she says yes. Perhaps the fact that both Rebekah and Isaac knew that God played such a large role in their coming together also fostered and strengthened their love for each other.

As I hinted in the introduction, we might picture this scene as forming the climax of a romantic comedy, with Rebecca and Isaac glimpsing each other in the distance and learning from the servants that this will be their spouse. The film might finish with a montage of their wedding and close-ups of them gazing lovingly at the other. But we read in the subsequent narrative that they experience challenges. I wonder if knowing that God brought them together helped them to endure the hardships.

Because God is love and loves us, he has made us to love. And these sweet snapshots of early romantic union can bring joy to our hearts. I invite you today to ponder the God of love and how he showers you with his affirmation and abundance.

God of belonging, you can bring together people in partnerships,
whether romantic or otherwise. Strengthen my love for you,
that I might love others better. Amen.

AMY BOUCHER PYE

A jostling within

Isaac prayed to the Lord on behalf of his wife, because she was childless. The Lord answered his prayer, and his wife Rebekah became pregnant. The babies jostled each other within her, and she said, 'Why is this happening to me?' So she went to enquire of the Lord. The Lord said to her, 'Two nations are in your womb, and two peoples from within you will be separated; one people will be stronger than the other, and the elder will serve the younger.' When the time came for her to give birth, there were twin boys in her womb. The first to come out was red, and his whole body was like a hairy garment; so they named him Esau. After this, his brother came out, with his hand grasping Esau's heel; so he was named Jacob.

The biblical narrative captures life after the storybook romance of Isaac and Rebekah. They, like Abraham and Sarah, contend with infertility, but God answered Isaac's prayers and Rebekah became pregnant. Note that while their infertility lasted nearly as long as that of Abraham and Sarah (20 years to the elders' 25), the narrator gives only one line to their longing, unlike the nine chapters in the earlier story. Perhaps the narrator in that lone verse assumes the accompanying heartache.

Although God answered Isaac's pleas, all would not be paradise with the growing family. The troubles between the twins are signified even before birth by their jostling of one against the other. Legend had it that Jacob and Esau tried to kill each other in the womb. And again the Lord will prefer the younger over the older, just as with Isaac and Ishmael.

We are not told why God favoured one child over the other, or why Isaac and Rebekah suffered for so many years before Rebekah fell pregnant. We can surmise that God strengthened their faith in him as they continued to seek his help, guidance and love, even as God strengthens our belief that he will follow through with his promises when he helps us to continue hoping and believing.

God of the impossible, I want to believe. Help me to hold onto your promises that you are faithful, good and loving. Amen.

AMY BOUCHER PYE

The power of hunger

The boys grew up, and Esau became a skilful hunter, a man of the open country, while Jacob was content to stay at home among the tents. Isaac, who had a taste for wild game, loved Esau, but Rebekah loved Jacob. Once when Jacob was cooking some stew, Esau came in from the open country, famished. He said to Jacob, 'Quick, let me have some of that red stew! I'm famished!' (That is why he was also called Edom.) Jacob replied, 'First sell me your birthright.' 'Look, I am about to die,' Esau said. 'What good is the birthright to me?' But Jacob said, 'Swear to me first'… So Esau despised his birthright.

'I'm so hungry I could die!' Do we ever utter these words, losing objectivity over what really matters when our physical needs take centre stage? We witness this phenomenon in Esau when he sold his birthright for a single bowl of lentil stew.

Note, as Martin Luther observed, that God had already promised this birthright to Jacob and that Esau did not actually have the right to sell it. But both were living according to their names, with Jacob deceiving his brother and Esau being concerned with things of the earth, such as this red stew.

With the preference of each of the parents for their favoured son highlighted in the text, we can assume that the reader would understand the significance of this split between members of the family. Yet the narrator does not comment on the wisdom – or lack thereof – of this kind of parenting style. We will, however, witness the continued effects of this division as the story progresses.

As we see here, God acknowledges the fragilities and failings of his people. The Bible is not a collection of elevated texts that ignore our physical requirements or relational missteps. Rather, our loving God bestows on us his grace, forgiveness and healing as he meets our physical, emotional and spiritual needs. And he can repair our broken relationships. We need only to turn to him.

Gracious God, please meet all my needs, those I acknowledge and those hidden to me. You are the source of all goodness and grace. Amen.

AMY BOUCHER PYE

Keeping promises

The Lord appeared to Isaac and said… 'Stay in this land for a while, and I will be with you and will bless you. For to you and your descendants I will give all these lands and will confirm the oath I swore to your father Abraham. I will make your descendants as numerous as the stars in the sky… because Abraham obeyed me and did everything I required of him'… When the men of that place asked him about his wife, he said, 'She is my sister,' because he was afraid to say, 'She is my wife.' He thought, 'The men of this place might kill me on account of Rebekah, because she is beautiful.'

Like father, like son. History repeats itself as Isaac, fearing the jealousy of the Philistine men, passes off his wife as his sister, just as Abraham, before him, had done with Sarah. Both Abraham and Isaac had travelled south towards Egypt and both made their wives available in Gerar. But God stepped in for both women and kept them from harm.

Before recounting this incident, the writer of Genesis shares how God repeats his covenant to Isaac, telling him not to travel outside the promised land and reaffirming that Isaac would have countless descendants. Through the stories that come before and after this confirmation of the covenant, the narrator emphasises that Isaac is not worthy of God's amazing blessing. But the writer also affirms that God will follow through on his promises, especially to honour Abraham's obedience.

The failings of this father/son duo could have had catastrophic effects on their wives, but God intervened. We see repeatedly in scripture how God looks out for the vulnerable and how he blesses those whom he loves.

If you face issues and challenges over which you struggle to believe that God will act, you could prayerfully imagine yourself in the story of Isaac and Rebekah in Gerar, putting yourself in Rebekah's place. Note the feelings and questions that arise within you as the story plays out, and how God responds.

God who loves the vulnerable and oppressed,
please act to save those who are in trouble and need.
Show me how I can be your hands and your feet on this earth. Amen.

AMY BOUCHER PYE

God's covenant

[Isaac] became rich, and his wealth continued to grow until he became very wealthy. He had so many flocks and herds and servants that the Philistines envied him… Isaac's servants dug in the valley and discovered a well of fresh water there. But the herdsmen of Gerar quarrelled with those of Isaac and said, 'The water is ours!'… He moved on from there and dug another well, and no one quarrelled over it… That night the Lord appeared to him and said, 'I am the God of your father Abraham. Do not be afraid, for I am with you; I will bless you and will increase the number of your descendants for the sake of my servant Abraham.'

The Lord made Isaac and his people prosper, but the accumulation of that wealth brought its own set of problems, namely the ire of the Philistines. With water a precious commodity, they quarrelled over the wells that Isaac dug. In fact, the Philistines were so aggravated that they filled up Isaac's wells, blocking the life-giving water. Amid this climate of recrimination and dispute, Isaac moved from place to place, fixing up the wells of his father and discovering fresh, running water. These discoveries were a sign that God was working behind the scenes.

Isaac must have needed to hear God's promises of blessing, because God made himself known to Isaac, affirming again the covenant he had made with Abraham. As Isaac faced strife and hardship, God wanted him to believe that he would come through for him. Isaac could trust in him.

The nomadic life would have taken a toll on God's people, but God revealed himself through these glimpses of grace. If they would notice and give thanks, even the ordinary things of water coming out of the ground could remind them of their caring God. Similarly we today can ask God to help us become aware of, and be grateful for, the way he meets our needs. Why not spend some time giving thanks for the ordinary things you might otherwise overlook, such as running water, heat, light and food.

'And my God will meet all your needs according to the riches of his glory in Christ Jesus' (Philippians 4:19).

AMY BOUCHER PYE

Plots and plans

'Are you really my son Esau?' he asked. 'I am,' he replied. Then he said, 'My son, bring me some of your game to eat, so that I may give you my blessing'... Isaac caught the smell of his clothes, he blessed him and said, 'Ah, the smell of my son is like the smell of a field that the Lord has blessed. May God give you heaven's dew and earth's richness – an abundance of grain and new wine. May nations serve you and peoples bow down to you. Be lord over your brothers, and may the sons of your mother bow down to you. May those who curse you be cursed and those who bless you be blessed.'

The lifelong division of brother against brother, fuelled by the parents, comes to a head at the end of Isaac's life. As he prepares to bless his favourite, the eldest, Rebekah overhears his plans and intervenes to release the blessing for her favourite, the youngest. She plots and plans, preparing Isaac's preferred dish and giving Jacob some animal skins so that the nearly blind Isaac will think that he is his hairy brother.

Her idea works and Isaac confers the blessing on the younger. Jacob, the deceiver, becomes the recipient of the covenant; God will continue his line through him, making his descendants to increase. Note the language of blessing echoes God's promises to Abraham, assuring him of abundant bounty from the earth.

From our point of view, it can feel unfair that the covenant is continued through trickery and falsehood. Although we might wince at the injustice of this situation, we can remind ourselves that actually neither Jacob nor Esau deserved the blessing anyway and that giving the blessing is God's prerogative.

Perhaps we can take a strange sort of comfort in knowing that God is not thwarted by this act of deception. After all, God is not limited by his creatures, and he can choose to bless and affirm people, however unworthy they are, including me and you.

Gracious God, thank you for forgiving me for the ways I deceive others and even myself. Help me to live in the light of your love, that I will reflect your goodness and grace. Amen.

AMY BOUCHER PYE

Family split

When Esau heard his father's words, he burst out with a loud and bitter cry and said to his father, 'Bless me – me too, my father!' But he said, 'Your brother came deceitfully and took your blessing.' Esau said, 'Isn't he rightly named Jacob?... He took my birthright, and now he's taken my blessing!' Then he asked, 'Haven't you reserved any blessing for me?'... His father Isaac answered him, 'Your dwelling will be away from the earth's richness, away from the dew of heaven above. You will live by the sword and you will serve your brother. But when you grow restless, you will throw his yoke from off your neck.' Esau held a grudge against Jacob because of the blessing his father had given him.

Now Esau is sorry. Earlier he gave away his birthright in a hunger-fuelled haze of need, and now that he has lost this prized inheritance, he is filled with regrets. The narrator says that this elder son weeps bitterly, but neither he nor his father can change what was done. The blessing will go to the younger son.

Isaac does not have much blessing left to give. Whereas for Jacob his blessings included enjoying heaven's dew and the earth's riches, for Esau he can only say that he will dwell away from the riches of the earth or the dew of heaven. Yet although he will have to serve his brother, he will not have to do so forever – at some point he will throw off the yoke around his neck. Words of cold comfort for the one deceived?

Bitterness and anger ensue as the strife between brothers deepens, with Esau wishing his brother dead. Jacob must leave the family home or risk bodily harm, and Rebekah realises that her plans may have worked but also have unintended consequences – she will have to live away from her favoured son.

As we reach the sad denouement of the story of Isaac, this longed-for answer to God's promise, we can reflect on the ways that we humans mess things up. And yet God does not give up on us.

Forgiving God, strike my heart with gratitude for the way you always call me back to you. Amen.

AMY BOUCHER PYE

Our loving God

Then Rebekah said to Isaac... 'If Jacob takes a wife from among the women of this land, from Hittite women like these, my life will not be worth living.' So Isaac called for Jacob and blessed him. Then he commanded him: 'Do not marry a Canaanite woman. Go at once to Paddan Aram... Take a wife for yourself there, from among the daughters of Laban... May God Almighty bless you and make you fruitful and increase your numbers until you become a community of peoples. May he give you and your descendants the blessing given to Abraham, so that you may take possession of the land where you now reside as a foreigner, the land God gave to Abraham.'

As the story of Isaac reaches its conclusion, we see the consequences of him and Rebekah not following God wholeheartedly. Both have to live without the day-to-day love of their favoured sons. Knowing that Jacob's life is endangered, Rebekah has Isaac send him away. Again, like Abraham, the father seeks a wife for his son from within their people group, but the son has to leave the land to find her.

As we read on, the narrative moves to Jacob and his journey with God, including his hip-changing dream. Thus far we have not witnessed him showing much faith in God or being a winsome character. But as he travels away from the family home, that changes.

Yet our focus has been on Isaac. He probably lived another ten years after giving his blessings to his sons. Did that decade include much laughter, the meaning of his name? We are not told. Nor do we learn if he and Rebekah expressed remorse for how they preferred one son to the other. We can hope that in their old age they reached peace with God and each other. We do see later how the brothers reconciled and buried Isaac together (see Genesis 35:27–29).

God's mercy prevails, and even though his people fail him, he will not give up on them. We can hold onto our faith in our loving God, trusting that however we mess up, he will never leave us.

Loving God, thank you for the story of these broken people whom you redeemed. Help me to receive and share your love. Amen.

AMY BOUCHER PYE

If you've enjoyed this set of reflections by **Amy Boucher Pye**, check out her books published with BRF Ministries, including...

Holding Onto Hope
*40 days of God's encouragement
through art and reflections*

978 1 80039 200 7
£12.99

To order, visit **brfonline.org.uk** or use the order form at the end.

Artificial intelligence: what does it have to do with me?

 Even if you are the greatest technophobe, it is worth recognising that everyone, everywhere is affected by artificial intelligence (AI). Whether going shopping or on a phone helpline, paying for parking or receiving healthcare, AI is already having an impact on your life and will increasingly do so in the coming years. Some of these technologies are extremely helpful. I am grateful that a chatbot can save me waiting half an hour to ask a simple question about my phone bill. On the other hand, I am concerned about the use of facial recognition software to track people's whereabouts in some countries.

As with most new technologies, the Bible has nothing to say about AI specifically, but much to say in general about how we use it. This series will equip you to think about how AI affects our lives and how we can use or respond to it. We will also ask: how are other people affected, and how can we speak up for them? How are the next generations using AI and how can we support them? We will explore broad biblical principles, such as being made in the image of God, idolatry, rest, the fall and what it means to be embodied. We will look at specific issues or aspects of human existence, such as creativity, exercising power, kindness and counselling.

These devotions have been written by a group of multitalented people from a wide variety of backgrounds.* Each has brought their own perspective to this very new topic. Some are more cautious than others about the potential of AI to contribute to society in particular ways. No doubt Christian thinking on this subject will develop rapidly, and a series like this will be very different in five or ten years' time. I hope that you are enlightened, challenged and inspired by these studies.

*Details on the individual contributors can be found in the 'Meet the authors' section on page 148.

RUTH BANCEWICZ, THE FARADAY INSTITUTE FOR SCIENCE AND RELIGION

Crowned with glory! Guided by AI?

When I consider your heavens, the work of your fingers, the moon and the stars, which you have set in place, what is mankind that you are mindful of them, human beings that you care for them? You have made them a little lower than the angels and crowned them with glory and honour. You made them rulers over the works of your hands; you put everything under their feet: all flocks and herds, and the animals of the wild, the birds in the sky, and the fish in the sea, all that swim the paths of the seas.

Just like David all those centuries ago, for most of us it is hard to gaze up at the glittering beauty of the night sky and *not* think in our heart, 'Somebody did this.' That somebody, our majestic God, has bestowed on you and me the honour and the responsibility to take care of his creation. Among all things, living or technological, it is only humans who are 'crowned with glory and honour' (v. 5). We alone are stewards. Could AI make us better stewards?

For example, self-driving cars could reduce emissions by 50% by identifying efficient routes and optimising driving speed. AI can analyse massive amounts of data from satellite images to project de-forestation or predict coastal communities at risk from flooding. AI is already used to diagnose cancers in humans, as well as diseases in plants and animals. All this benefits both us and 'the flocks and herds... birds in the sky, and the fish in the sea' (vv. 7–8). There is much to celebrate.

But AI also introduces us to new responsibilities. For example, as technology enables us to live longer, we become subject to 'new illnesses' like Alzheimer's, which previous generations rarely encountered. Are we prepared to help those communities at risk of flooding? Furthermore, AI itself could pose an environmental risk, as the associated computing could generate CO_2 emissions akin to the aviation industry.

AI will bring huge opportunities to help care for our world, but with it new responsibilities.

---

*Lord strengthen my commitment to care for this extraordinary world.
As new technologies appear, I pray we have the wisdom and foresight to
use them for good. Amen.*

CHRIS GOSWAMI

Embodied

Long ago God spoke to our ancestors in many and various ways by the prophets, but in these last days he has spoken to us by a Son, whom he appointed heir of all things, through whom he also created the worlds. He is the reflection of God's glory and the exact imprint of God's very being, and he sustains all things by his powerful word. When he had made purification for sins, he sat down at the right hand of the Majesty on high, having become as much superior to angels as the name he has inherited is more excellent than theirs.

This stunning opening to the book of Hebrews tells us that Christ's ministry is vast in scope, yet deeply embodied – from creating and sustaining worlds, to suffering and dying on the cross, and then being raised to sit down in the heights of Majesty. In all this, Christ embodies God's glory, showing us who God is. God's glory is not distant and uncaring. Instead, Christ in all his world-shaping power gives himself up to make his people clean.

Because of Christ's purifying work, we can share in his embodied ministry. However, our lives increasingly revolve around routines that lack deep engagement – scrolling on social media, news websites or online shopping apps. Many of these habits depend on AI systems. For example, companies may use AI to highlight attention-grabbing content based on past user behaviour or to monitor and drive workers' productivity.

AI promises instant solutions but tends to keep us glued to our screens, feeling distracted and overwhelmed. We can end up ignoring and demeaning our own embodiment, leading to inaction or even reinforcement of harmful behaviours. These patterns stand in contrast with Christ's self-giving, purifying participation in creation.

AI systems can be extremely useful tools for connecting us to the needs of the world. By prayerfully orienting routines in light of Christ's embodiment of God's glory, we can put AI in its proper place and make room for ourselves and those around us to engage deeply and constructively with God, the world and each other.

Father, may Christ's embodied revelation of you startle us and orient our use of technology for your glory. Amen.

RACHEL SIOW ROBERTSON

The image of God

So God created humans in his image, in the image of God he created them; male and female he created them. God blessed them, and God said to them, 'Be fruitful and multiply and fill the earth and subdue it and have dominion over the fish of the sea and over the birds of the air and over every living thing that moves upon the earth.'

The Bible tells us that God and people are somehow alike. We are created in God's image. This does not mean that God has a body like ours – as if God has fingers, hair and a liver. Instead, we share in God's character.

One way we share God's character is through our use of language. As we saw yesterday, Hebrews reminds us that God has spoken 'in various ways' (Hebrews 1:1, NIV). When we use language, we reveal God's image. We also demonstrate God's likeness in forming relationships. God longs to relate to his people, and we are most fully alive when we relate to one another.

Recent advances in artificial intelligence have enabled machines to do many of these things. AI can communicate using language. We may even feel as if we have a relationship with a chatbot. So, is AI also in God's image?

Not when it comes to language. A toddler may say 'sorry', but not feel remorse or even sound apologetic. It is the same with AI. Although the words may look right, there is no genuine feeling – or even meaning. Relationships are most authentic when we see things from the other person's point of view. This was the point of the incarnation of Jesus. In Christ, God knows the world from the human perspective. A machine will never know what it is to be human. It can never have a real relationship with us.

AI can never show God's image and likeness. Only humans can do that. We are wonderfully and uniquely made.

Creator God, the psalmist reminds us that you have made us little lower than the angels and crowned us with glory and honour.
Thank you for the gifts of creativity, language and relationships.
Help us to use each one to bring glory to you. Amen.

TIM BULL

AI and gardening

The Lord God took the man and put him in the Garden of Eden to work it and take care of it. And the Lord God commanded the man, 'You are free to eat from any tree in the garden; but you must not eat from the tree of the knowledge of good and evil, for when you eat from it you will certainly die.'

Regardless of our job or role in society, we are all, at our core, gardeners – cultivators of the world. I am not much of a literal gardener myself, but I know that gardening consists of fulfilling two equally important tasks: releasing potential and maintaining the conditions of flourishing.

Our core purpose is to 'work' the garden of the world, releasing its abundant potential for all to enjoy. Alas, extraction and exploitation have been a dominant story in our world. We are equally called to 'take care of' the garden, fostering the conditions of flourishing and fruitfulness with reverent care.

Throughout history, humans have crafted tools. From spears and ploughs to steam engines and computers, tools have increased human force and capability. We have used them both to work and to exploit the garden of the world, to nurture and to undermine the conditions of flourishing.

With the arrival of increasingly capable AI systems and other so-called frontier technologies, our fundamental purpose remains the same. As in the past, we can release potential and nurture 'the life of the world', rather than exploit our neighbours and extract from creation. Yet the challenge is steeper because of the unprecedented power of our latest tools.

How might you use a powerful AI assistant to bless others and bring out the best of them? If you are, say, a teacher, you might use AI to help craft an engaging lesson that will stretch and delight your pupils. If you work in the corporate sector, an AI assistant might help finally organise your life and release precious time to give to your church community, family and friends.

Father God, please help me to discern what I can do to help ensure that AI and other cutting-edge tools are used to release rather than extract potential, to nurture rather than destroy the conditions of flourishing for all your creatures. Amen.

NATHAN MLADIN

55

Fallen

When the woman saw that the fruit of the tree was good for food and pleasing to the eye, and also desirable for gaining wisdom, she took some and ate it. She also gave some to her husband, who was with her, and he ate it. Then the eyes of both of them were opened, and they realised they were naked; so they sewed fig leaves together and made coverings for themselves. Then the man and his wife heard the sound of the Lord God as he was walking in the garden in the cool of the day, and they hid from the Lord God among the trees of the garden.

Artificial intelligence systems are tools, and like any other tools humankind has crafted, they can work for or against us. AI tools created by organisations and governments will not be perfect, as we ourselves are imperfect fallen beings.

AI tools are powerful: the organisations behind them have the potential to know a lot about us, to be ubiquitous, as AIs are increasingly 'present' in multiple kinds of devices, and to make decisions about us or on our behalf. AI systems have been empowered by humans (and their data) to recommend, predict, select and decide. As access to these tools are not equitably distributed, they have the potential to divide humanity into 'the haves' and 'the have nots' digitally, socially, even politically, and physically. This means AI can discriminate based on existing human biases and further entrench existing systemic societal inequalities.

God's position has not changed. God is still omniscient, omnipresent and omnipotent. So when God says, 'Do not fear, for I am with you' (Isaiah 41:10), 'Do not conform to the pattern of this world, but be transformed by the renewing of your mind' (Romans 12:2), and 'Seek justice. Defend the oppressed' (Isaiah 1:17), he means it!

Father, help us to not fear AI or the power that it could wield. Give us your wisdom and discernment as to when, how and why we use AI tools. Use our ability to think critically and to challenge what we see, as well as decisions about people that are made autonomously or augmented using artificial intelligence. Amen.

PATRICIA SHAW

Work and rest

And on the seventh day God finished his work which he had done, and he rested on the seventh day from all his work which he had done. So God blessed the seventh day and hallowed it, because on it God rested from all his work which he had done in creation.

When Michael Schluter set up the secular Keep Sunday Special campaign in 1985, it was widely believed that all-week trading would damage families, communities and local economies. Meanwhile the Lord's Day Observance Society (now known as Day One Christian Ministries) campaigned for no Sunday working on the Christian sabbath – the day of rest. The Jewish sabbath is Saturday – the last day of the week – and the fourth commandment relates to it (Exodus 20:8). The biblical rationale makes sense of the secular need for restful time and the secular argument chimes with the biblical imperative. Yet we now live in a seven-day-a-week, 24/7 world.

Why did God rest on the seventh day? For humanity, rest is about stopping and stepping out of the routine, just sleeping sometimes. Whether it is physical, mental or pastoral labour, well-being requires a break from it. Yet God's rest is also about contemplation: to comprehend and appreciate. One can be so engrossed in work that there is no rest for reflection. Unable to reflect from within the task, one needs to pause and survey. This is purposeful rest. St Benedict called prayer the 'work of God', but prayer is simultaneously, paradoxically perhaps, a form of rest too.

If AI is going to ease workloads and give us more time, the godly purpose of that time is something which many people increasingly say they have no time for: prayer. AI gives an opportunity to rest in the Lord and work at prayer.

The time AI will save is a gift for some. God built time for restful reflection into the created order. AI may yet release and enhance that gracious gift by which we can contemplate faith and life and, through prayer, build on our relationship with God, Father, Son and Holy Spirit.

God, help us always to take time to rest in you and truly appreciate your wonderful work as creator, redeemer and sustainer. Amen.

GORDON GILES

Idolatry

The carpenter… plants a cedar and the rain nourishes it… Half of it he burns in the fire; over this half he roasts meat, eats it, and is satisfied. He also warms himself and says, 'Ah, I am warm by the fire!' The rest of it he makes into a god, his idol, bows down to it and worships it; he prays to it and says, 'Save me, for you are my god!'

I am certain artificial intelligence will be as revolutionary as the microscope. As a neuroscientist and consultant neurologist, I see the potential for AI to analyse vast amounts of data in a way that was impossible ten years ago, or to improve the diagnostic accuracy of scans by limiting human error. However, we must not be dazzled by its potential and must always retain a sense of perspective. Yes, it can process data at vast speeds, but AI will never have the empathy, understanding and humanity of a scientist or clinician.

Idols from scripture may seem very remote from our own experience, but it is worth remembering that idols were objects that were created by a people seeking an alternative to God's gifts and blessings. They became blinded by the craftsman's skill, placing their trust in these objects rather than God.

AI is a tool that we can (and should) use positively, but when we see AI as a 'better' alternative to the skills and empathy of humanity, whether it is in healthcare or science, we are at risk of placing our faith in this man-made tool and celebrating it above God's creation. If we do this, we too become guilty of the idolatry described in scripture, using microchips and computer code rather than wood like the carpenter in Isaiah.

We can be thankful for AI and the change it will bring to our lives, but we must also remember that it will never surpass the beauty and wonder of God's creation. If we suggest otherwise, we risk creating a new idol for our modern world and forgetting the warning of Isaiah, which still resonates strongly today.

Lord, grant us the grace to celebrate the developments in science that you have gifted to us and the humility to recognise these tools are nothing compared to the beauty and wonder of your creation. Amen.

IAN MORRISON

Begotten

This is the written account of Adam's family line. When God created mankind, he made them in the likeness of God. He created them male and female and blessed them. And he named them 'Mankind' when they were created. When Adam had lived 130 years, he had a son in his own likeness, in his own image; and he named him Seth.

The Bible teaches that human beings are created in God's image. So some people have suggested that when we humans invent AI machines, we are somehow creating new beings in our own image. But our passage shows that Adam passes on the mysterious image and likeness of God, not in what he makes, but in the child that he fathers. The Hebrew word *yalad*, rendered by the NIV as 'having a son', is translated in the Authorised Version with the old English word 'begot'. Just as the Son was 'begotten not made' (in the words of the Nicene Creed), so in biblical thinking the same applies to our biological children. They also are 'begotten not made'. We pass on the image of God to the children we beget.

When we *make* something it is a product of our will, it is different from us and it is ours to control. But when we beget a child, this new and wonderful being is not a product of our will, but a gift from our nature. He or she is fundamentally the same as us, and, as every parent learns, we are not able to control and direct our children. We must set them free to be themselves.

So, however sophisticated and powerful AI machines may become, we must always remember that they are designed and produced by human beings; they are a product of human choices and intentions. Machines are not free to follow their own path. A healthy relationship with AI depends on understanding that humans define what AI means and what role it should play in society. When used with wisdom, AI can help us to flourish, but it can never replace us.

Father, thank you that your precious image is passed on to the next generation as we beget children. Teach us to develop a healthy relationship with AI that helps us to flourish and become the people you meant us to be. Amen.

JOHN WYATT

The Third Sunday before Lent 59

Manners matter

Better to be despised and have produce, than to be self-important and lack food. The righteous know the needs of their animals, but the mercy of the wicked is cruel. Those who till their land will have plenty of food, but those who follow worthless pursuits have no sense.

'Manners makyth man.' The politeness, respect and courtesy which make up good manners are essential to humanity in the building and restoring of relationships. The character of a person is determined not only by the attitude they have but also by how they treat people and things that they deem lesser or weaker than them. So does it matter how we treat an AI machine?

Proverbs 12:10 makes reference to humans and animals, both of which were created in service to God, and the stewardship responsibility of humanity is to respect and care for God's creation. How we treat animals matters, and how we relate to each other is equally important. There is need for compassionate consideration and kindness by adopting a way of thinking and doing that evidences our practical and moral responsibility. Sadly, the attitude of the wicked is described as cruel – lacking any sense of gentleness, kindness or consideration to things, let alone people.

In a world with created technology advancing exponentially, AI-powered systems are not only influencing the way we live or think, but in some aspects they reflect our attitudes and behaviour. While Chatbot technology, such as ChatGPT, or virtual assistants, like Alexa, Cortana, Bixby, Siri and Google Assistant, are not able to process human emotions at the moment, they use AI algorithms for speech recognition, to understand language processing, answering questions quicker than humans can through expert systems, performing tasks like setting reminders, playing our favourite music or providing us direction using polite and courteous voice tones.

Is it possible that when we are harsh, rude and impatient with virtual assistants, these tendencies creep in to how we treat or communicate with others? How are these observed behaviours teaching children to be polite and considerate to others, including AI-powered systems?

Lord, make me an instrument of kindness, being compassionate and well-mannered with all I meet, in all I say and all I do. Amen.

CHARMAINE MHLANGA

Creativity

The Lord spoke to Moses, 'See, I have called by name Bezalel son of Uri son of Hur, of the tribe of Judah, and I have filled him with a divine spirit, with ability, intelligence, and knowledge, and every kind of skill, to devise artistic designs, to work in gold, silver, and bronze, in cutting stones for setting, and in carving wood, to work in every kind of craft. Moreover, I have appointed with him Oholiab son of Ahisamach, of the tribe of Dan; and I have given skill to all the skilful, so that they may make all that I have commanded you.

Machines have already 'turned their hands' to a variety of art forms. Computer-generated poetry has been around for decades. Algorithms are regularly used to compose new music. In 2022 the humanoid robot, Ai-Da, painted a portrait of the late Queen Elizabeth II.

Bezalel and Oholiab received God-given gifts of human creativity. Through the power of the Holy Spirit, they became skilled artists. They were commissioned to put their gifts to work in the service of God, at the time when a tabernacle was being constructed in his name.

As machines become increasingly able to mimic human creativity, we face a choice. We can yield that ground to manufactured devices. We surrender the realms of poetry, conversation, painting and music. We retreat into ever smaller arenas in which to express talents which machines cannot yet mimic.

Or we choose a different route. We decide that whatever creativity may be mimicked, we have a God-given call to be creative. The Holy Spirit invites us to know his empowering as we seek to flourish as the creative beings God calls us to become.

We all have different perspectives on our own creative abilities, and on whether or not we view AI as a tool to enhance those gifts. Whatever those perspectives, we are all made in God's image, and so all designed to be creative in turn. We are all called to use that creativity in his service.

Lord, we thank you for your awesome gifts of creativity within us.
Give us wisdom that we may release those gifts for your glory.
In Jesus' name. Amen.

JUSTIN TOMKINS

61

Comforting words

Praise the Lord. How good it is to sing praises to our God, how pleasant and fitting to praise him!... He heals the broken-hearted and binds up their wounds. He determines the number of the stars and calls them each by name. Great is our Lord and mighty in power; his understanding has no limit. The Lord sustains the humble but casts the wicked to the ground. Sing to the Lord with grateful praise; make music to our God on the harp.

One of the earliest uses of AI was in cognitive behavioural therapy, which has been shown to be effective in the treatment of anxiety, depression and a range of other issues. Problematic behaviours are 'challenged' using exercises, experiments, and so on, with the goal of learning about the relationship with harmful thoughts and behaviours and ultimately reducing their occurrence. Therapists quickly realised that aspects of this process could be automated, using simple forms of AI to generate questions, responses and challenges.

Should we as Christians put our faith in AI in this way? While we value the skills and abilities of professionally trained counsellors, for many of us our first recourse when facing challenging times and situations may be to seek solace and advice from trusted friends or pastors. We may be advised to seek additional help from professionals (AI-augmented or otherwise) where appropriate. We also know, in our hearts, that God is the one to whom we can turn at any time.

However well trained, AI – like humans – will sometimes fall short. Scripture often reminds us, as in this psalm, of both the great gentleness and yet awesome power of the Lord. God is the one who never fails. The one who is able to carefully bind our wounds when we need to be cared for is also the awesome one, who knows the names of all the stars in the universe.

Infinitely wise as well as being endlessly caring, God is the only one whose understanding is limitless.

'God himself will be with them and be their God. "He will wipe every tear from their eyes. There will be no more death" or mourning or crying or pain, for the old order of things has passed away' (Revelation 21:3b–4).

MURDO MACDONALD

Protectors

'And for your lifeblood I will surely demand an accounting. I will demand an accounting from every animal. And from each human being, too, I will demand an accounting for the life of another human being. Whoever sheds human blood, by humans shall their blood be shed; for in the image of God has God made mankind.'

Genesis 9 describes God's re-creation of the world. The creation was 'very good' (Genesis 1:31), but that did not last. Sin had taken hold, leading to murder (Genesis 3—4). The wickedness became so great that God resolved to put an end to all people (Genesis 6). We then come to the aftermath of the flood and God's second creation.

There are many echoes of the first creation – separating dry land from water, the reappearance of plants, the repopulation of the world with animals, a command for Noah and his sons to be fruitful and increase in number. But there is a difference. God has to spell out the value of human life and the punishment for murder. God has made us in his image; human life is very precious and to be treated with respect.

God still permits shedding blood, not least as Joshua led the Israelites into the promised land. There are times when we still need armed forces and when taking human life is the lesser of two evils, but we will be held to account. These are not decisions to be delegated casually to automated systems. Autonomous weapons that identify hostile targets and eliminate them without human intervention are very attractive to the military and law-enforcement agencies. Very cost-effective as they are, God will demand an accounting for the life of another human from their operators.

Blood is precious to God in this re-creation. The rainbow calls us to peace while reminding us of God's love, love ultimately fulfilled in the blood of Jesus on the cross that guarantees our place in the new creation that is to come.

Lord God, thank you for making us in your image. Please help us to respect that image faithfully and responsibly in a fallen world. Amen.

PETER ROBINSON

Incarnated teaching

Therefore go and make disciples of all nations, baptising them in the name of the Father and of the Son and of the Holy Spirit, and teaching them to obey everything I have commanded you. And surely I am with you always, to the very end of the age.

Modern technology is amazing. Google can tell you almost anything you want to know. Whatever question my kids have, ChatGPT can tell them an answer in less time than it takes me to look up from my cup of tea and ask them to repeat themselves. If technology puts all possible information in the palm of your hand, what do we – mere human beings – have to offer the next generation, or any generation? Much in every way!

Jesus' instruction to his disciples is not to *tell* people, so that they know information. Rather, it is to *teach* people, so that they obey his commands. Jesus commands us, for example, to love one another. The simplest AI can tell a person to obey Jesus' command to love; it takes only a few words. But what does it take to teach someone to obey Jesus' command to love?

It takes a life that shows that it is possible, day after day, year after year, to be kind, gracious, forgiving, patient, self-controlled and hopeful. Not simply *saying* that it is possible, but *showing* that it is possible. It may take being awake at 3.00 am, holding a person's hand as we identify with their suffering, weeping bitterly with them, sharing silent recognition that words will not do and that none of the nice, neat answers make any sense. Teaching to love requires showing that in real, messy life, you love. And you continue to love even when you stand to lose everything you hold dear, because that is how obedience to the command works.

God places great significance in humans. We are divinely called to a task that cannot be accomplished by anything else. We can let technology tell. But we must not think that this does away with our task to teach.

God, thank you for the place that you have given to humanity in your plan for building your kingdom. Amen.

MIKE BROWNNUTT

Increasingly human

Now the Lord is the Spirit, and where the Spirit of the Lord is, there is freedom. And all of us, with unveiled faces, seeing the glory of the Lord as though reflected in a mirror, are being transformed into the same image from one degree of glory to another, for this comes from the Lord, the Spirit.

AI is humanity's most powerful tool, the first in history that seems able to make decisions and create new ideas by itself. The latest chatbots' responses are so human-like, it is easy to feel confused about the nature of our relationship with AI. But while amazingly capable and clever, AI chatbots are really only simulating a human response, predicting the most probable next word based on having absorbed vast quantities of human writing and online content. AI is but a pale reflection of humanity when compared against the eternal 'glory of the Lord' in whose image we are beautifully and wonderfully made.

Today's passage reminds us of our freedom in Christ – freedom to be allowed into the presence of God and freedom to be transformed ever more deeply into his likeness by his Spirit. Unlike an artificial intelligence, God has given us the ability to love, to enjoy deep relationship with him and our fellow humans, to be self-aware and to be able to contemplate our place in his universe. It is in relationship with God and our fellow humans that we find true meaning and value, not in pseudo-relationships with AI entities which reflect back our own desires and leave us open to manipulation.

It is important to be informed about AI, the great opportunities for society and the risks of harm, and to be comfortable to engage with technology as a tool to serve and help humanity. But we can also encourage one another that relationship fulfilment is found in our freedom to love and worship God, who knows and cares for us deeply, and in the gift of loving relationships with other humans made in his image.

Thank you, Lord, that I am intimately known and loved by you and am being continuously transformed into your likeness through the saving grace of Christ. Help me to engage with technology in a healthy way. Amen.

GRAHAM BUDD

Joel

Picture the scene:the apostle Peter stands to address the crowd in Jerusalem. The Holy Spirit has just fallen on the disciples of Jesus at the first Pentecost with great effect. 'Fellow Jews and all of you who live in Jerusalem,' Peter says, 'let me explain this to you.' And right away he quotes five verses, no less, from the prophet Joel.

Why Joel? After all, Peter had the entire Hebrew scriptures to choose from. What is so special about this prophet, just three chapters, mostly in poetry, sandwiched in our Bibles between Hosea and Amos? It is possible that the risen Jesus had used this text in preparing his disciples for the outpouring of the Spirit on all people. As we will see this week, there is one prophecy from Joel which seems to stand him out from all the other Old Testament prophets, a game-changer of cosmic significance.

We know hardly anything about Joel, just his name (which means 'the Lord is God') and his father's name. We don't know when or where he lived. There are some tantalising clues but nothing definite. What we do know is that Joel was immersed in the Hebrew scriptures, what we know as the Old Testament. He alludes to and quotes from the prophets Isaiah, Jeremiah, Ezekiel, Amos, Obadiah, Nahum, Zephaniah, Zechariah and Malachi, as well as sharing passages we find in Exodus and even Genesis. This reliance on so much scripture suggests a later date for this remarkable prophet, possibly towards the end of the Old Testament period.

Clearly Joel has a profound and extensive knowledge of scripture, and this informs his understanding of how God works in his world, not least through his chosen people. Through his reading of scripture, he understands that God is a God of mercy and so, however bleak the setting, there is always hope.

And furthermore, he recognises that God abounds in steadfast love, always willing to bless, invariably longing to forgive. We are assured of a glorious future, not just for Joel's own people, not just for all people, but for the entire created order. You cannot get any bigger than that. A major prophecy from a minor prophet!

ROSS MOUGHTIN

Be real

The word of the Lord that came to Joel son of Pethuel: Hear this, O elders; give ear, all inhabitants of the land! Has such a thing happened in your days or in the days of your ancestors? Tell your children of it, and let your children tell their children, and their children another generation. What the cutting locust left, the swarming locust has eaten; what the swarming locust left, the hopping locust has eaten; and what the hopping locust left, the destroying locust has eaten.

The entire nation is in crisis, overwhelmed with a disaster that has shaken it to the core. 'The fields are devastated, the ground mourns' (Joel 1:10). Even the temple in Jerusalem has stopped functioning: 'the grain offering and the drink offering are cut off' (v. 9). A powerful army has invaded the land, destroying everything in its path – an army of locusts, vast and voracious. Nothing escapes its assault: 'It has laid waste my vines and splintered my fig trees' (v. 7, RSV). There is more: a prolonged, scorching drought: 'Pomegranate, palm, and apple – all the trees of the field are dried up.' As a result, 'surely, joy withers away among the people' (v. 12).

Like many people, I try to block off any painful experience, to bury any painful memories. But nothing is gained by denying reality. Like Joel, we need to face it head on; we need to ask God to help us to see him in what is happening. Here we draw strength from his presence even in our perplexity. It can take courage.

Such is the extent and depth of this calamity, unmatched by any previous tragedy, that Joel begins his prophecy by urging his people with their leaders to remember this throughout future generations. Here he reverses the usual directive of prophets to recall God's wonderful acts of mercy, especially the rescue of his people from slavery in Egypt. So the prophet summons his people to lament, the priests to mourn.

Joel needs to make sense of what is happening, so he looks to the Hebrew scriptures to help him understand where God is in this catastrophe. He has every confidence that God will speak to his people. Like them, we need to be prepared to listen, so important when we cry out to God for help.

Lord, help me to confront my fears. Amen.

ROSS MOUGHTIN

When the foundations shake

Consecrate a fast; call a solemn assembly. Gather the elders and all the inhabitants of the land to the house of the Lord your God, and cry out to the Lord. Alas for the day! For the day of the Lord is near, and as destruction from the Almighty it comes. Is not the food cut off before our eyes, joy and gladness from the house of our God?

Such is this crisis that Joel summons his people along with their leaders to come together at the temple in Jerusalem, first of all to fast. 'Come, pass the night in sackcloth, you ministers of my God!' (Joel 1:13). Here they are to meet with God, their God, on his terms not theirs. It is a painful but necessary step if his people are to experience God's support during these dark days. After all, God, named by Joel as *Shaddai*, the Almighty, is more powerful than any enemy that would menace them.

Look at the extent of the destruction around you, the prophet urges: 'Even the wild animals cry to you [Lord] because the watercourses are dried up' (v. 20). And here Joel makes the astonishing claim as he addresses the people of Israel: *their distress is from God himself.*

For this is no ordinary crisis. Joel declares that this is 'the day of the Lord' (v. 15). Earlier prophets, especially Isaiah and Amos, had taught that this is when God intervenes decisively in his nation's life to confront injustice and challenge his people. It is in no way a comfortable experience, but it is necessary if God's people are to be true to their calling. If they are to be his people to convey his blessing to the world, they need to repent of their disobedience and decide to honour God.

So Joel leads his people in prayer, honest and heartfelt. They have no alternative, as he explains, 'for fire has devoured the pastures of the wilderness, and flames have burned all the trees of the field' (v. 19). Sometimes we turn to God only when the ground underneath our feet is being shaken, only to discover that it is God who is shaking it. Like Joel, we need to turn to him in penitence and be open to whatever God may say to us.

To you, O Lord, I cry. Amen.

ROSS MOUGHTIN

No ordinary army

Blow the trumpet in Zion; sound the alarm on my holy mountain! Let all the inhabitants of the land tremble, for the day of the Lord is coming, it is near – a day of darkness and gloom, a day of clouds and thick darkness! Like blackness spread upon the mountains, a great and powerful army comes; their like has never been from of old, nor will be again after them in ages to come. Fire devours in front of them, and behind them a flame burns. Before them the land is like the garden of Eden, but after them a desolate wilderness, and nothing escapes them.

'Everyone, get ready!' Joel summons his people to battle through the blast of the ram's horn. A mighty army threatens his people with total devastation, even God's good land. Everyone is terrified.

But this is no ordinary army laying waste everything before them. The prophet Joel is able to see that the locust army represents something more sinister, even more dangerous. It is as if they are real warriors, disciplined and determined: 'They leap upon the city; they run upon the walls; they climb up into the houses; they enter through the windows like a thief' (v. 9). Furthermore, the prophet uses cosmic imagery to suggest that this terrifying invasion is of a different order altogether. 'The sun and the moon are darkened, and the stars withdraw their shining' (v. 10).

Who is at the head of this massive invasion force? 'The Lord utters his voice at the head of his army; how vast is his host!' God himself is coming to judge his people, such is their disobedience, and there is simply no escape, no hope of resistance. 'Truly the day of the Lord is great, terrible indeed – who can endure it?' (v. 11).

Unusually for a prophet, Joel does not identify among his people any particular sin or act of defiance against God. Their disobedience is pervasive, their rebellion ongoing. The very fact that God is speaking to his people through his prophet is a ground for hope. They need to understand what is happening and understand God's purpose. Only then will they be able to respond aright.

Lord, keep us alert, to see your purpose even in tough times. Amen.

ROSS MOUGHTIN

God's grace, our only hope

Yet even now, says the Lord, return to me with all your heart, with fasting, with weeping, and with mourning; rend your hearts and not your clothing. Return to the Lord your God, for he is gracious and merciful, slow to anger, abounding in steadfast love, and relenting from punishment. Who knows whether he will not turn and relent and leave a blessing behind him, a grain offering and a drink offering for the Lord your God?

Now we hear God himself speaking directly to his people. 'Yet even now' (v. 12): even when your complete destruction seems inevitable, even when you have reached the very limit of your endurance; even now, when all seems lost, find hope in this hopeless situation. The reason is simple: God is 'gracious and merciful, slow to anger, and abounding in steadfast love' (v. 13).

So Joel urges his people to return to God. He is 'the Lord, your God' forgiving their disloyalty and committed to their protection. Here the prophet refers to the scriptures, in particular the passage in which God forgave his people after they had worshipped the golden calf during the exodus from Egypt. There we read that it is in God's very nature to show mercy, even when his people dishonour and disobey him.

Joel calls his nation to repent and return to their Lord. But he knew his people only too well. 'Rend your hearts and not your clothing,' he says (v. 13). Their repentance has to be real, heartfelt. God looks for a genuine change, for his people to stop being selfish and start living for him. Sadly – as we all know – it is so easy to go through the motions to get what we want.

'Who knows whether he will not turn and relent?' (v. 14). That is, we must not presume upon God's forgiveness. His willingness to forgive and start afresh is always a gift of sheer grace. Even the offerings his people may bring to the temple are in reality not a gift to him but a gift which he himself graciously supplies.

God, we resolve to rely on you alone and not on our own resources. Amen.

ROSS MOUGHTIN

When God restores

O children of Zion, be glad, and rejoice in the Lord your God, for he has given the early rain for your vindication; he has poured down for you abundant rain, the early and the later rain, as before. The threshing floors shall be full of grain; the vats shall overflow with wine and oil. I will repay you for the years that the swarming locust has eaten, the hopper, the destroyer, and the cutter, my great army that I sent against you.

Now everything changes. Joel's message of disaster and desolation becomes one of joy and celebration as God purposes to restore the years that locusts have eaten. At the prophet's urging, the people do repent and resolve to honour the Lord their God. 'Then the Lord became jealous for his land, and had pity on his people' (Joel 2:18). Joel uses God's covenant name, 'the Lord', to show his special relationship with Israel; he becomes *jealous*, because God is passionate for their response.

So the rain falls and a bountiful harvest is to be reaped. No more will his people be a laughing stock among the nations. God promises prosperity and peace; all enemies are vanquished, his army withdrawn. His *shalom* prevails: 'I am sending you grain, wine, and oil, and you will be satisfied' (v. 19). The 'day of the Lord' now becomes a day of rich blessing, such is the intensity of God's love for his people.

There is now no need to be afraid. Here Joel addresses not only his people but the entire land, even literally: 'Do not fear, O soil; be glad and rejoice, for the Lord has done great things! Do not fear, you animals of the field, for the pastures of the wilderness are green' (v. 21). Joel's vision is for the entire land, people and animals, rain and soil. God's shalom is expansive and all-encompassing. Joel thinks big, for the simple reason that he worships a big God.

There is more: God promises his very presence with his people. His covenant relationship with the people of Israel is now restored. 'You shall know that I am in the midst of Israel and that I, the Lord, am your God and there is no other' (v. 27).

We have not great faith in God but faith in a great God.

ROSS MOUGHTIN

An amazing prophecy

Then afterward I will pour out my spirit on all flesh; your sons and your daughters shall prophesy, your old men shall dream dreams, and your young men shall see visions. Even on the male and female slaves, in those days I will pour out my spirit. I will show portents in the heavens and on the earth, blood and fire and columns of smoke… Then everyone who calls on the name of the Lord shall be saved.

There is more, much more. It is not just that God promises prosperity to his fearful people, not just that he promises to be with them; he promises to be with them in a new and special way. As the culmination of the 'day of the Lord', God promises to pour his Spirit, even his life-giving presence, on all flesh. This is something totally new, even unexpected, and so Joel must explain what this means. No longer will God's gift of prophecy, the ministry of speaking out in his name, be given to a few select individuals for a particular purpose at a specific time. No longer will just a special few be shown visions by God. This gift of his Spirit is for everyone.

Earlier prophets, such as Ezekiel and Zechariah, had anticipated this giving of God's Spirit but only to the house of Israel. Now Joel extends this wonderful prophecy to 'all flesh'. Such is the significance of this day that even the cosmic order is shaken 'before the great and terrible day of the Lord comes' (v. 31). Those who have God's spirit will be secure.

Joel spells it out: not only men but women too, not only the old and experienced but the young and immature, not only the privileged rich but those who are in slavery, exploited and abandoned. Everyone. No wonder the apostle Peter quotes Joel by name to the crowd at Pentecost: 'His prophecy is being fulfilled now!'

Yet his promise is even bigger than that. Joel anticipates the time when God's Spirit, even his breath, is poured out onto 'all flesh', which means what it says: every living creature. A breath-taking vision for God's glorious future, but not yet.

'Let everything that breathes praise the Lord!' (Psalm 150:6). Amen.

ROSS MOUGHTIN

God is on the move

The Lord roars from Zion and utters his voice from Jerusalem, and the heavens and the earth shake. But the Lord is a refuge for his people, a stronghold for the people of Israel. So you shall know that I, the Lord your God, dwell in Zion, my holy mountain. And Jerusalem shall be holy, and strangers shall never again pass through it. In that day the mountains shall drip sweet wine, the hills shall flow with milk, and all the streambeds of Judah shall flow with water; a fountain shall come forth from the house of the Lord and water the Wadi Shittim.

Like the army of locusts, surrounding nations menace the people of Judah. They have looted the temple at Jerusalem and even sold their children into slavery to faraway lands. Their tumult is deafening, altogether intimidating: 'Multitudes, multitudes, in the valley of decision!'

Nevertheless, their din is no match for God, who roars from his holy temple, summoning his people for battle, reversing the familiar prophecy: 'Beat your ploughshares into swords, and your pruning hooks into spears; let the weakling say, "I am a warrior"' (Joel 3:10). Such is the Lord's empowerment.

Now God is on the move to confront evil among all the nations and to bring his justice so as to right all those wrongs wrought against his people. For the 'day of the Lord' is a day of justice, a day of huge significance when 'the sun and the moon are darkened, and the stars withdraw their shining' (v. 15). At a time when his people feel particularly vulnerable, Joel proclaims God's protection; the Lord is their refuge, their stronghold. No more will Jerusalem the holy city be defenceless to every passing army.

We began this week with withered vines and a parched land. Now fertility abounds and from his holy temple God waters the entire land with rich blessings. Thus the prophecy of Joel ends with a note of triumph: 'For the Lord dwells in Zion' (v. 21)!

The message of Joel is that God is with his people, however bleak their outlook. For this prophet the whole witness of scripture points to God's steadfast love and thus a glorious future for all people. Simply repent, he urges, and resolve to live by his amazing promises.

God, we rejoice in your amazing faithfulness. Amen.

ROSS MOUGHTIN

To win the world for Christ: Romans 7—11

 Before we plough into the middle of Paul's lengthy letters to those first Christians in Rome, let us take a brief look at the context. We do not know exactly how the news of Jesus Christ arrived in Rome, but Acts 2:10 offers a clue. At Pentecost, when the Holy Spirit empowered the witnesses of Jesus' death and resurrection to burst onto the streets of Jerusalem with the message of salvation, Acts 2:10 recalls that 'visitors from Rome' were present. When those 'visitors' returned home, they would have been eager to share their Jerusalem experience. Most probably Peter had travelled to support this emerging group of Christian Jews and Gentiles, but Paul, ever the Pharisee, wanted to make sure new Gentile believers were grounded in Jewish scripture. His letter determined to set before the Roman Christians his legalistic, logical arguments for faith in Jesus Christ as the Son of God. Unlike his other letters, Paul addressed people he had never met, nor would ever meet face to face. It was a time of relative freedom for a variety of beliefs before the onset of persecution of God-fearers in Rome.

Do not be put off by the somewhat heavy, convoluted, doctrinal language. Instead, feel the driven zeal of this man of letters, catch his desperation to win the world for his Lord. Paul was a man of an age staggeringly different to our own. His letter is strewn with verses from his scripture, our Old Testament, to persuade and support his arguments. Martin Luther, the great German reformer, called this letter to the Romans 'truly the purest gospel'.

These deeply theological chapters include some of the most sublime verses in our Bible which, over the centuries, have given strength, hope and comfort to millions. The Mediterranean world in the first century AD had deep racial suspicions, religious segregation and division of wealth and power. Paul's letter was, and is, a clarion call to the universal, inclusive love of God. It is a statement so badly needed today.

Although we begin with Romans 7, I can think of no better introduction than Paul gave in his own introduction to ancient believers at the heart of the greatest empire of that time: 'Grace to you and peace from God our Father and the Lord Jesus Christ' (Romans 1:7, NRSV).

ELIZABETH RUNDLE

Leave your past behind

Do you not know, brothers and sisters – for I am speaking to those who know the law… a married woman is bound by the law to her husband as long as he lives, but if her husband dies, she is discharged from the law concerning the husband… In the same way, my brothers and sisters, you have died to the law through the body of Christ… so that we are enslaved in the newness of the Spirit and not in the oldness of the written code.

My last sail on the Sea of Galilee was 'captained' by a delightful Orthodox Jew. In November the days were getting shorter. When we landed, this devout man rushed to buy bread for Shabbat before sunset. By Orthodox rules he was not allowed to buy bread, or anything, once the sun had set on the sabbath. Was he a slave to the law?

Paul was a man bursting with Pharisaic interpretation of Moses' law but revisiting that law in the light of the death and resurrection of Jesus Christ. The coming of God's Messiah had given new meaning to the law, and Paul's personal encounter with Jesus on the road to Damascus had thrown his understanding upside down.

No longer was the Christian a slave to the law from duty or fear, but released through Jesus' death into a new and right relationship with God and other people. Paul wrote to people, the majority of whom were Jews, who would not have found his argument as confusing as we do in our very different world. That is not to say they would have found it easy to accept. Think about the change to peoples' lives and attitudes when they fall in love – or at the birth of a baby: old self-indulgences give way to embracing and living for another. We have a change of heart. We change and grow as we become followers of Christ. Is that what Paul is meaning here?

In essence Paul was pointing out the old way had worked for their 'then' but, as followers of Jesus Christ, they lived in a new 'now'. The old ways had served their purpose, a foundation on which to build their 'new life of the Spirit'.

Have you had experiences to change your thinking?

ELIZABETH RUNDLE

Paul's personal anguish

I do not do what I want, but I do the very thing I hate… in fact it is no longer I who do it but sin that dwells within me… For I do not do the good I want, but the evil I do not want… Wretched person that I am! Who will rescue me from this body of death? Thanks be to God through Jesus Christ our Lord!

How honest! Paul, the proud Pharisee opens up about his inner conflicts in a most unexpected way. I warm to him here as he gives a glimpse into his personal struggles. Paul described the battle within his inmost self more openly than any other apostle. His direct analysis of the age-old turmoil between right and wrong, body, mind and spirit is disarming. Suddenly he comes across as more 'human', more 'accessible', more like us! Do we not all have times of struggle? Have we not all experienced that sinking feeling of failure? This is so much more than a miserable 'mea culpa'. Paul pronounces a solution – the Lord Jesus will rescue us from the bonds of 'self'. Before Moses' law, people were free to do as they liked without recrimination. However, once they had received the law, they had a framework by which to recognise good from evil.

I love the television programme *Saving Lives at Sea*. Regardless of their age, people manage to find myriad ways of getting into trouble on the water. Just when they are carried by currents or injured and terrified, along speeds the lifeboat. These volunteer men and women do not yell at the person or condemn them, and they often risk themselves to rescue people. It is hard to admit we need help. It is painful to assess our own mistakes, failings and turmoil.

Today, our world appears in complete turmoil. Individual lives stranded in an ocean of physical enticements and compulsive social media. It is as though winds of indifference have become destructive cyclones with hearts and lives broken on the rocks of grief and isolation. Prayer is the Christian's 'Mayday'. Paul knew Jesus was his rock and his salvation, and he channelled all his energies into sharing this fact as widely as possible.

What is your 'Mayday' shout today?

ELIZABETH RUNDLE

Groans of creation

We know that the whole creation has been groaning together as it suffers together the pains of labour, and not only the creation, but we ourselves, who have the first fruits of the Spirit, groan inwardly while we wait for adoption, the redemption of our bodies. For in hope we were saved. Now hope that is seen is not hope... But if we hope for what we do not see, we wait for it with patience.

In this century more than any other, voices are raised concerning the plight of our rivers, oceans and lands. Creation is truly groaning; often it is yelling out in pain. This pain inevitably reflects in human relationships. Tragically as we look around, change, decay and heartache spoil God's phenomenal creation, this amazing planet – including you and me. On a much smaller scale, Paul addressed the same idea and then, catching the people's mood, he lifted them with the word 'hope'. That small word holds enormous scope and substance.

How often do you use that word? We tend to say things like 'Hope you are well', 'Hope my team wins', 'Hope to see you soon'. All are genuine expressions of hope for future success and happiness. Hope used to be a popular girls' name and for each baby born, anywhere in the world, they are automatically surrounded by the hopes of those who love them. Just think about it – *you* were once the centre of hope. Paul's words are hard on our 21st-century ears, mixing the past, present and future of salvation. However, the whole tenor of his writing was to help and encourage and to impress upon new believers that accepting the law of love in Jesus Christ meant they would be included in God's family. That family includes us!

In purely physical terms, creation flourishes when treated with love and respect. Surely the nations could live in peace and prosperity if they pursued the way of peace and co-operation. This has been the hope of Christians and most faiths. Paul adds the word 'patience' – such a necessary gift of the spirit. Is there a particular need for which you want to pray?

How can we best treat all creation with respect, patience and love?

ELIZABETH RUNDLE

Ash Wednesday

Likewise the Spirit helps us in our weakness, for we do not know how to pray as we ought, but that very Spirit intercedes with groanings too deep for words. And God, who searches the heart, knows what is the mind of the Spirit, because the Spirit intercedes for the saints according to the will of God.

Lent 2025 begins: only six-and-a-half weeks to Easter! Long before contemporary interest in secular meditation, cosmetic fasting and life re-appraisal, Christians favoured the weeks prior to Easter celebrations for self-denial, prayer and studying the Bible. The period of 40 days was founded on the biblical account of Jesus fasting in the wilderness before the start of his earthly ministry. It was also the custom for early converts to fast and pray prior to their baptism.

Many years after Paul had written to Roman congregations, the practice of being anointed with ash became a solemn part of Ash Wednesday. Ash is mentioned in both Old and New Testaments as a symbol of repentance. Even though the word 'repentance' has long gone out of fashion, our world is desperately in need of recapturing its true essence. The Hebrew word, *teshuvah*, literally means to turn back to something you have strayed away from. So Lent offers a golden opportunity to sort ourselves out, physically, emotionally and spiritually: a special gift of time for deepening our faith and understanding.

With all the devastating situations around the world today, as well as traumatic events in the lives of those we know and love, it is almost impossible to know how to pray. Paul reminded his first readers, and those who have encountered these words since, that it is okay to be lost for words. A simple sigh will suffice. Sighs and tears are an international language.

I approach Ash Wednesday as a serious fixture in the calendar. In busy days it is too easy to overlook our need for a spiritual reality check. So I encourage you to embrace this symbolic gesture. Seek a closer walk with our Lord who took time out to ready himself for all that lay ahead. We do not know what lies ahead for us, but we can be assured Christ is with us.

In what way does Ash Wednesday help to deepen your faith?

ELIZABETH RUNDLE

More than conquerors

Who will separate us from the love of Christ? Will affliction or distress or persecution or famine or nakedness or peril or sword?… For I am convinced that neither death, nor life, nor angels, nor rulers, nor things present, nor things to come… nor anything else in all creation will be able to separate us from the love of God in Christ Jesus our Lord.

Do you know a more impassioned statement of personal faith? From my own experience, these verses are among the most uncomplicated, heartfelt words Paul ever wrote. Above the trials, tragedies and sufferings we see and experience, it feels as if Paul is waving an enormous banner of encourage-ment. On this banner, in my imagination, bold letters a mile high shine with the word *Nothing*. After all his hardships – from shipwreck to imprisonment, from rejection to the 'thorn in his flesh' – this apostle to the Gentiles declares nothing in the whole wide world would separate him from his Lord.

Let us remember the recipients of this letter: a mixture of Jews and Gentiles, men and women, wealthy and struggling, some highly educated and many of lesser opportunities and attainments. They are a reflection of any gathering in any part of the world, in any century, including our own communities.

Paul reasons, argues and makes bold statements to illustrate the new spiritual life versus the old self-centred life. Basically he puts forward a stark choice. Those who accept God's love in Jesus have an assurance that all things will work for good. Whatever happens, nothing we have to face or endure, not even death, can break the bond of love with God in Jesus Christ. Surely, these are some of the greatest inspirational words in all his letters. Yet they remain as hard to embrace as when they were first written.

Lent is our time for spiritual self-appraisal. Perhaps we have far more knowledge of 'sin' in the world than original Roman Christians. Wars, devas-tation, disease and the suffering of the innocent dishearten and cloud our resolve. But today, give thanks to God for those people, those 'saints' who have shown remarkable, indestructible faith in adversity. They shine in our lives as beacons of God's love in our hurting world.

Try reading Romans 8:35–39 replacing 'us' with 'me'.

ELIZABETH RUNDLE

If only...

I have great sorrow and unceasing anguish in my heart. For I could wish that I myself were accursed and cut off from Christ for the sake of my own brothers and sisters... They are Israelites, and to them belong the adoption, the glory, the covenants, the giving of the law... the promises; to them belong the patriarchs, and from them, according to the flesh, comes the Christ, who is over all, God blessed forever. Amen.

Paul tells it as he sees it. To support his view, he trawls scripture for evidence. This is his legalistic mind justifying the truth in his eyes and heart.

Are you proud of your ancestors? Delving into family history has given me a broad brushstroke of people whose DNA I have inherited. Agricultural labourers and glove-makers, sawyers and servants, they are however distant and hazy figures in the past. To Paul, though, scripture was a living history, his connection to the great icons of faith a cause for immense pride. Yet he was distraught knowing that Jesus had been rejected by his own people – Paul's own people. It was an impossible paradox. So Paul alights upon a thread which becomes a justification. He states the distinction was not between Jew and Gentile, but between those who accepted and those who rejected the promised Messiah. Devastated at his own peoples' rejection of God's Messiah, he used scripture to show how several famous names in Jewish history had also deviated from true worship. He was so desperate for the Jews to accept the Messiah, he was even willing to cut himself off from Christ to win them to the gospel truth.

In Paul's mind, the Jews had everything going for them. The Lord God had made sacred covenants and promises which had shaped the worship and thinking of the nation. How could they not realise?

How interesting it is that this cry of frustration follows one of Paul's great statements of faith. It shows even people with the firmest faith are not immune to depression. Many have walked a similar path. It is a desolate cry of, 'If only'. How different a million circumstances would be 'if only' hearts would accept the person of Jesus Christ.

Who do you long to see accept Jesus Christ into their life?

ELIZABETH RUNDLE

Pottery lesson

But who indeed are you, a human, to argue with God? Will what is moulded say to the one who moulds it, 'Why have you made me like this?' Has the potter no right over the clay, to make out of the same lump one object for special use and another for ordinary use?

I have only once sat at a potter's wheel. My immediate reaction: it is not as easy as it looks! My concentrated effort produced a small pot. On one side it looked passable, but turn it round and the drastic sag showed it was an obvious failure. I needed to begin again.

Taking the illustration of one of the oldest of crafts, Paul's message is, for once, crystal clear. None of us is perfect, but in God's hands we believe we can be made new, accepted, forgiven and loved by the God of all time. It is an ideal illustration, as everyone knew about pottery and would have understood his analogy.

The latter half of Romans 9 wrestles with the fact that the creator God can love his creation even if they are not descended from Abraham. Being a man of his time and religious attitude, Paul refers to other, non-Jewish, ethnicities as being like objects 'for ordinary use'. Paul turned back to the great prophets, to Isaiah and Hosea to justify his explanation of the inclusivity of God's love. The prophets' words had been written hundreds of years previously but, as is the case today, familiar words are not always taken seriously, especially if they do not quite fit our own ideals.

For the Gentile converts in Rome this was welcome, heart-changing teaching. For those of Jewish heritage it was almost impossible to accept. Here we come face to face with a trio of ugly attitudes – superiority, prejudice and segregation. To us these verses are convoluted and over-zealous, but for Paul, his message was life or death: life in faith or death to salvation offered by Jesus Christ. By every means possible his only aim was to win the world for his Saviour.

'Have thine own way, Lord. Thou art the potter, I am the clay; mould me and make me after thy will, while I am waiting, yielded and still'
(Adelaide Pollard, 1862–1934).

ELIZABETH RUNDLE

The stumbling block

What then are we to say? Gentiles, who did not strive for righteousness, have attained it, that is, righteousness through faith, but Israel, who did strive for the law of righteousness, did not attain that law… They have stumbled over the stumbling stone, as it is written, 'See, I am laying in Zion a stone that will make people stumble, a rock that will make them fall.'

How different words appear when written rather than spoken. Those same words can be transformed when we see the person's face and hear the tone of speech. It is like that with Paul's letters. To a synagogue gathering, this was about the most unpopular, provocative statement, bordering on blasphemy. I sense a sharp intake of breath as those words hung in the air, yet try to imagine Paul's face as he pleads his Lord's cause.

The sad theme repeated throughout his nation's history was one of rejection, renewal, then rejection, culminating in Paul's time in the rejection of God's promised Messiah. Most Pharisees and teachers of the law (of Moses) had choked humanity and compassion out of the law to such an extent that it had become a source of pride in themselves rather than a response to God's guidance and love.

The region of Israel/Palestine is a land of stone; it was natural to link God with indestructible rocks and stones. But stones also illustrate hardened, inflexible hearts. On the other hand, when someone wants to heap praise on a person, they often use the phrase 'They are my rock.'

Let us pick our way through ancient thoughts and language. Paul implored people to accept Jesus as God's Son, the Messiah for all people, by faith not by rigid observance of works. No one, however 'good' they are, can earn their way to faith. In this period of Lent, many people look to give up something they enjoy as a mark of piety. Paul's words make it plain: *striving* to be good misses the point. Faith comes from our *personal acceptance* of Jesus Christ, our rock and foundation for a new and right relationship with our Lord in this life and beyond.

Thank God today for the person who has been a dependable rock for you.

ELIZABETH RUNDLE

Jesus is Lord!

For Christ is the culmination of the law so that there may be righteousness for everyone who believes... If you confess with your mouth that Jesus is Lord and believe in your heart that God raised him from the dead, you will be saved... For there is no distinction between Jew and Greek; the same Lord is Lord of all.

Tiny, insignificant words often have an unsettling way of stopping us in our tracks. Two such little words appear in today's reading: 'if' and 'all'. 'If' I do not water pot plants, they will die – that leaves the choice and responsibility to me. On the other hand, the word 'all' is non-negotiable. However much choice we exercise in our daily life, when it comes to faith in Jesus as Lord, we cannot pick and choose just the bits that suit us. Nor can we pick and choose who else will also honour Jesus. In this context, 'all' embraces everyone.

Through the centuries Paul's letter has provoked both joy and consternation. It was, and is, uncomfortable and challenging. Our human instincts are rooted in the group, be it family, community or ethnicity, so for many, widening these horizons can be intimidating. At best, anything new or different is likely to raise simmering anxieties. Remember, Paul was the evangelist to the Gentiles. This was strikingly new. His timeless message that *all* were welcome and included in God's family through Jesus Christ offers each individual a connection with God.

Being the fulfilment of 'the law', Jesus opened the way for us to find the right attitude to each other and to our Lord. Not some kind of goody-goody exterior face, but a genuine compassion from the heart. I wonder if, sometimes, we feel it is our responsibility to bring people to know Jesus as Lord, rather than accepting it as the work of the Holy Spirit?

'Jesus is Lord' is regarded as the earliest form of Christian creed. It may have been the required declaration as converts entered their new community of faith at baptism.

'Christ doth call one and all... new-born worlds rise and adore' (Joachim Neander, 1650–80). Think of how you would express a creed for anyone entering your Christian community.

ELIZABETH RUNDLE

Pass it on…

How are they to believe in one of whom they have never heard? And how are they to hear without someone to proclaim him? And how are they to proclaim him unless they are sent? … So faith comes from what is heard, and what is heard comes through the word of Christ. But I ask, have they not heard? Indeed they have… Of Israel he says, 'All day long I have held out my hands to a disobedient and contrary people.'

'Have you had a kindness shown? Pass it on!' Opening and encouraging words from an old American gospel song, the tune of which was composed by George Stebbins (1846–1945). I have a feeling the song writer and traveller and the great letter-writer and traveller Paul would have had much in common. In the 1890s, Stebbins and his wife were part of a mission to India. He wrote and sang for missions to Egypt, Palestine, Rome, Paris and London. Like Paul, George's life was spent in sharing his faith in Jesus, his Saviour. Both men took the message of the risen Saviour to people in different countries without thought for themselves.

The message, which applies to each and every Christian, carries the obligation to pass on the good news of Jesus Christ. It is funny how we do not need prompting to pass on happy news of marriages and births, promotions or holiday adventures, and bad news spreads like wildfire. Sharing faith is another matter.

Paul wrote to mixed groups. Some knew Hebrew scripture but the majority knew little or nothing about the Messiah. Modern communication is a miracle, yet the best way of making Jesus Christ known is still person to person by attitude and example. There are times when we can all be 'disobedient and contrary people' (v. 21), but you would not be reading these notes if your heart had not been stirred by the Holy Spirit. Sometimes Paul thumped out his message in harsh tones, while George Stebbins sang his message with tunes to lodge in peoples' hearts. Each one of us is given opportunities to live out our faith by example and – pass it on!

Who is the person with whom God wants you to pass on your faith?

ELIZABETH RUNDLE

You are never alone

I ask, then, has God rejected his people? By no means! I myself am an Israelite, a descendent of Abraham, a member of the tribe of Benjamin. God has not rejected his people whom he foreknew. Do you not know what the scripture says of Elijah, how he pleads with God…?

Delving into our ancestry has become an intriguing hobby, but most of us know very little about those in our genealogies. Beyond the recent past, our forebears are distant figures who do not impinge on our lives.

Not so with Paul. He spoke with enormous pride in his ancestry and the great characters of the nation's past were held as 'living' illustrations to bolster his reasoning. Paul expected the Christians in Rome to know their scripture, and Elijah was an ideal example. I love the story of Elijah. He was so consumed with his own situation he had fallen into deep depression and hopelessness. He felt abandoned. However, the lesson from Elijah was that he was not on his own. Paul highlighted this to show it is people who leave God; God never leaves his people.

From time to time, random polls are taken across Generation Z to gauge their knowledge of history. These polls reveal that among that group not everyone is knowledgeable of or even interested in historic events. If we take that view towards Paul's audience, his words fall into place. Prophetic voices repeatedly called the nation for commitment to God's guidance, but their words had largely gone unheeded. That was not to say God had forsaken them, but to infer there was always a faithful remnant. In these verses Paul elaborated the theme which is both old and new: a relationship with God is not the entitlement of an individual, group or nation, but God's free gift of grace to each open, trusting heart.

When I entered ministerial training, a wonderful mentor advised me: 'Never say you do not have enough time, and never say you do not have enough resources.' Think about your own situation. Have you ever felt isolated in a group? Have you ever felt God was absent in your life? Take time today to recognise you are not on your own.

Lord Jesus, in simple trust, I open my heart to you. Amen.

ELIZABETH RUNDLE

Root and branch

Now I am speaking to you gentiles... If the part of the dough offered as first fruits is holy, then the whole batch is holy; and if the root is holy, then the branches also are holy... Remember: you do not support the root, but the root supports you.

When you look around your home, is there anything that Paul and the people of his time would recognise? Simple furniture, crockery, and tools and utensils would be familiar, but that is about all. However, when it comes to natural things – even with modern dietary requirements and with the sparse greenery of high-rise cityscapes – Paul's analogy of dough and trees retains a timeless, universal reference point. Down through the centuries, Paul points us to everyday, physical features to press home his message of spiritual needs.

This is not dancing on a pin; this is a highly intellectual man on a world-embracing mission. Recurring throughout these intense letters Paul wove themes of warning, hope and unity. Like us, though, Paul could not encapsulate the mystery of God's grace, forgiveness and inclusive love. That divine mystery is beyond human conception, but not beyond human acceptance.

Paul spoke, thought and wrote with the innate pride of the Pharisee, and for all his appeal as an apostle to the Gentiles, nevertheless he was rooted in his heredity. He was steeped in the custom of offering 'shewbread' in the holy of holies. This was the symbolic acknowledgement and thanksgiving for God giving and sustaining life. And it is interesting that bread is central in the Eucharist or Holy Communion. Paul viewed the faraway gatherings of believers in Jesus Christ as 'branches', and we all know how branches can be blown down in a gale or show signs of die-back.

Today we are bombarded with a plethora of television and radio programmes and thousands of books on cooking and gardening. We should all be experts! Olive trees, so common all around the Mediterranean countries, now make popular centrepieces for small gardens and courtyards. Mine grows healthily in sandy, heathland soil, but I know if the root is damaged the tree will suffer. You are God's tender plant.

In what ways can you, as a branch, support others?

ELIZABETH RUNDLE

Getting to the point

I want you to understand this mystery, brothers and sisters, so that you may not claim to be wiser than you are: a hardening has come upon part of Israel until the full number of the gentiles has come in. And in this way all Israel will be saved: as it is written, 'Out of Zion will come the Deliverer… And this is my covenant with them, when I take away their sins.'

Children are not always patient in listening to explanations. Many teachers watch understanding nods, when all those nods really mean is 'Yes, yes, get on with it!' We become easily bored by repetition and quickly lose interest. Was Paul trying to retain attention to his message before people shrugged in disinterest?

Let us examine the essence of this argument. He refers once more to the prophet Isaiah and the prophesy that God's Messiah, the deliverer, will come from Zion, that is, from God's own people. The apostle obviously struggled with the horror that the Messiah had been rejected by his own people. It is worth remembering that Paul himself had been the arch-persecutor of those first believers in Jesus as the Messiah (Acts 8:3). It is highly likely that this was the reason for Paul's repetitive, often desperate, persuasiveness. Paul longed for every nation to honour Jesus as Lord and Saviour, with those who had previously hardened their hearts being welcomed back into God's family.

Another important strand is Paul's mention of the covenant. The Lord God had made successive covenants, or promise-bonds, which over the centuries culminated in the life, death and resurrection of Jesus Christ. Covenants were sacred, and God's promises stood as the foundation for the divine and human relationship. Jesus, the Messiah, embodied the covenant, and his death paved the way for our forgiveness. The Christian is embraced within the promises, which, to Paul, was overwhelming, wonderful news, like the mystery of resurrection itself.

Paul wrote as a prophet because Jesus had spoken directly to him. However much people in Israel rejected the Messiah (even he himself!), he boldly claimed that 'all' would be saved.

What does being saved mean to your life?

ELIZABETH RUNDLE

Doxology

O the depth of the riches and wisdom and knowledge of God! How unsearchable are his judgements and how inscrutable his ways! 'For who has known the mind of the Lord? Or who has been his counsellor?' 'Or who has given a gift to him, to receive a gift in return?' For from him and through him and to him are all things. To him be the glory forever. Amen.

In several Bibles, these verses are headed 'Doxology'. It reminds us that books within the Bible are a mixture of narrative and poetry. At the end of this chapter, and the close of our notes on this portion of Paul's letter to Rome, he combines lines from the prophet Isaiah (40:13) and Job (41:11).

It feels as if Paul had exhausted his arguments, and I imagine him momentarily staring into the distance while his scribe, Tertius, waited, quill poised. What was left to say but this admittance that God is beyond description, beyond criticism and understanding, yet who deserves all our worship and praise. These verses come as a kind of relief after all the sometimes harsh words and theological contortions. However, before we leave this section, it would be good to reflect on the particular message singing out to the world in these words: mercy, covenant, resurrection, love. However inadequately we try to sum up this part of Paul's letter, these words are indeed the root of Christian faith. They shine into the world, and into our lives with beams of hope.

We could exchange three of those four words with contemporary language: forgiveness, promise, new life. The unsearchable, inscrutable creative power that is God, promises forgiveness and new beginnings through Jesus Christ. As we draw closer to Easter and trace the path Jesus took to the cross, we are reminded that, 'God so loved the world that he gave his only Son, so that everyone who believes in him may not perish but may have eternal life' (John 3:16). This was Paul's urgent message to the immediate recipients of his letters. In mystery and miracle it is also the urgent message for the whole world today.

Can you echo: 'Throughout all time and in all places,
to God be the glory. Amen'?

ELIZABETH RUNDLE

Wilderness psalms: Psalms 30—40

In this series of readings, we focus on Psalms 30—40, all of which are attributed to David. We know that he was described as the 'sweet psalmist of Israel' and that God inspired him to write many of the songs in the book of Psalms (2 Samuel 23:1, KJV).

These particular psalms come from the period in David's life before he became king in Israel, when he was on the run from Saul in the wilderness, with many enemies. He often hid in the desert, fearful for his life, but David's response was always the same. He would turn to God with his sorrows, lift his heart up to the Lord and cry for the Lord's help. Out of his adversity he has left us a lasting legacy of deep spiritual truth and words which we can use to approach God in our own times of stress and anxiety. His honesty and humility shine through. There is no attempt to maintain an image of perfection. His relationship with God is open and frank. We see David in his raw humanity, which helps us to accept our own flawed and frail selves.

Several themes shine through these songs. One is that of *trust*, the belief that God will hear and answer prayer and eventually bring his deliverance. This seems to me to be what Christian living is all about, hanging on to God in childlike faith when all around us is in turmoil. Allied to this is the idea of *waiting*, waiting for God to act and for his timing to come to pass. It is in our waiting that we learn patience, that most elusive of virtues. Yet another theme is that of *praise and thanksgiving*, sometimes before prayer is answered, sometimes afterwards. Gratitude should characterise God's people because we are recipients of so much goodness, but sadly we often forget what God has done.

Finally, notice the *presence of Jesus*, who is referred to several times prophetically and who quoted from these psalms in his own ministry. He was soaked in the psalms, and that in itself is an incentive for us to spend time immersed in these ancient hymns.

Look out for these recurring ideas, and more. May you be blessed as you read.

TONY HORSFALL

Joy in the morning

I will exalt you, Lord, for you lifted me out of the depths and did not let my enemies gloat over me. Lord my God, I called to you for help, and you healed me... Sing the praises of the Lord, you his faithful people; praise his holy name. For his anger lasts only for a moment, but his favour lasts a lifetime; weeping may stay for the night, but rejoicing comes in the morning.

Although this psalm is said to have been written for the dedication of the temple, it is more likely to have been David's palace or house that he had in mind. Either way, an occasion for thanksgiving and reflection on the faithfulness of God presents David with an opportunity to share his testimony with the assembled guests. What God has done for him, he can do for all.

We are not told the specifics of the situation, but what is clear is that David was in dire straits and needed divine assistance. He had become proud and complacent, and God humbled him. In his moment of need, though, he cried out for help, and God reached down and rescued him. His sorrow was turned to joy, his mourning to dancing, and praise filled his heart.

The abiding lesson is that even though we go through times of tearful loss and deep sadness when we can see no way through, the darkness will not last forever. Joy will come in the morning because God is faithful.

Our response to God's intervention in our lives is threefold. First, it is appropriate to give thanks to him, to sing his praises and rejoice in his mercy towards us. We cannot keep silent before God's goodness. Second, it is right to seek opportunities to tell others about the grace we have received, to share our story with them so that their faith is strengthened. Third, we should never take his favour for granted but walk humbly with him.

Lord, help me to trust you in my times of darkness and give me grace to hold on to your promises. You are faithful. You have helped me before, and you will help me now. Amen.

TONY HORSFALL

The wonders of his love

In you, Lord, I have taken refuge; let me never be put to shame; deliver me in your righteousness. Turn you ear to me, come quickly to my rescue; be my rock of refuge, a strong fortress to save me… Keep me from the trap that is set for me, for you are my refuge. Into your hands I commit my spirit; deliver me, Lord, my faithful God.

You may well recognise the words of trust in this psalm (v. 5), which were echoed by Jesus on the cross: 'Jesus called out with a loud voice, "Father, into your hands I commit my spirit." When he had said this, he breathed his last' (Luke 23:46).

I am encouraged to know that in this moment of extreme need, Jesus was fortified by recalling the words of scripture and this particular psalm, which he clearly knew well. Notice he makes his declaration of faith with a loud voice, defiantly shouting its truth into the darkness that was seeking to engulf him. And notice too, he begins with a word not used in the psalm, but so often on his lips – 'Father'. His trust is placed securely not in some impersonal force, but in his heavenly Father who he knows will bring him through the darkness of death.

Both David and Jesus testify that God is worthy of our trust, yet trust is not always easy. In the deep darkness of bereavement and loss some years ago, I could see no hope for the future. I tried earnestly to trust God, but no matter how hard I tried I knew I was not trusting him and still felt afraid and uncertain.

Then, in conversation with a friend, I suddenly realised that my trust was not the issue. What mattered was that God is trustworthy. Whether I trusted him or not, he would remain faithful and would bring me through – 'If we are faithless, he remains faithful, for he cannot disown himself' (2 Timothy 2:13). Once I grasped this I relaxed and found I did trust God, because it was about him and not me.

Why not meditate on these precious words: 'Father, into your hands I commit my spirit'?

TONY HORSFALL

Forgiveness and fellowship

Blessed is the one whose transgressions are forgiven, whose sins are covered. Blessed is the one whose sin the Lord does not count against them and in whose spirit is no deceit. When I kept silent my bones wasted away... Then I acknowledged my sin to you and did not cover up my iniquity. I said, 'I will confess my transgressions to the Lord.' And you forgave the guilt of my sin.

Where can true happiness be found? In a world that craves excitement and thrills, yet seems never to be totally content, David reminds us that only in relationship with God can lasting peace be found. It is the blessing of knowing we are forgiven and restored to fellowship with God that we need above all else if we are to thrive as human beings.

Sin creates a dislocation not only with God but also within us. Breaking God's laws leads to a troubled conscience, and guilt and shame. These painful emotions in turn can cause a dis-ease within our bodies, especially if we try to hide our sin. Only in confessing our sin to God can we find the relief that comes with knowing we are forgiven.

God deals with sin, not by pretending it doesn't matter, but by providing a 'covering' for it. In Old Testament times this was done through the sacrificial system, but these find their complete fulfilment in the sacrificial death of Jesus on the cross, by which our sins were dealt with once and for all. Paul quotes verses 1–2 as confirmation that this blessing is a gift of grace, given freely to all who trust in God for forgiveness (Romans 4:4–8).

Being forgiven in this way opens up for us a life of fellowship with God. Not only are we reconnected to God, but we learn to walk with him through life, listening to his voice and following where he leads us on the adventure of faith (vv. 8–9).

Lord, no one is immune from the pull of sin, even the most seasoned followers of Jesus. Thank you that forgiveness is freely available. Help me to keep my conscience clear and my heart always open to receive your forgiveness. Amen.

TONY HORSFALL

Waiting in hope

**For the word of the Lord is right and true; he is faithful in all he does…
By the word of the Lord the heavens were made, their starry host by the
breath of his mouth… For he spoke, and it came to be; he commanded,
and it stood firm… We wait in hope for the Lord; he is our help and our
shield.**

Nowadays we are used to instant responses. We can order something online,
and it will be with us the next day. We send a text and expect an immediate
reply. We are impatient if we get held up in traffic, frustrated if our train is late.

The life of faith does not work like this, however, and the apparent
slowness of God is a cause of difficulty for many. We expect God to answer
our prayers immediately and for situations to change quickly. If things do
not happen rapidly, we conclude that either God did not hear us or our
prayers are in vain.

Waiting is a common theme throughout the psalms, and we see it here.
There is no doubt that God is our helper and that he is worthy of our trust.
His word of promise can be relied upon, for he is a faithful God and his word
has power – in creation he spoke and things came into being. But his timing is often different to ours. God is never in a hurry and makes all things
beautiful *in his time* (Ecclesiastes 3:11). Trusting God therefore requires us
to wait patiently for God to act.

God uses times of waiting to strengthen our desire. If we are serious
about our prayers, we will persevere in our asking and not give up at the
first sign of delay. Waiting develops our faith, for we are forced to rest in
the character of God and trust in his reliability. The joy of answered prayer
is sweeter for the waiting, more appreciated and valued.

---

*Lord, I know you are at work in me, ridding me of my immature
demandingness and creating in me a mature, restful confidence in you.
Help me to cooperate with you in my waiting. Amen.*

TONY HORSFALL

Taste and see

**I will extol the Lord at all times; his praise will always be on my lips...
I sought the Lord, and he answered me; he delivered me from all my fears.
Those who look to him are radiant; their faces are never covered with
shame. This poor man called, and the Lord heard him; he saved him out
of all his troubles... Taste and see that the Lord is good; blessed is the
one who takes refuge in him.**

This psalm comes from a specific situation in David's life when he sought
refuge with the Philistine king Achish. When his true identity became known,
David feigned madness and was sent away, finding refuge in the cave of
Adullam (1 Samuel 21:10—22:1).

David is full of praise for his deliverance, calling others to join him in
celebration. His song is an acrostic, each sentence beginning with successive letters of the Hebrew alphabet. In particular, David invites those who
are afflicted and in trouble to experience for themselves that God is good
and takes care of his people.

The principle of 'taste and see' is a tried and tested one. Have you been
in a supermarket and been invited to taste fresh bread from the bakery? It
tastes wonderful, and you immediately think, 'I'll buy a loaf of that.' Personal
experience convinces you of the quality of the offer being made.

Today, God invites us to 'taste' what is on offer through the gospel, and to
'see' for ourselves that he is good, faithful and caring. How will you respond?

Perhaps you feel broken-hearted (v. 18). Perhaps your world has fallen
apart. Maybe a marriage has ended, a loved one has died, your hopes have
been shattered. Yet David says that God is close to those whose hearts ache
with pain. You are not alone, he is there with you in all the mess, giving hope.

Perhaps you feel crushed in your spirit. Life has knocked the stuffing out
of you. The demands on you are overwhelming, the pressure unsustain-
able. You are ready to give up. David reminds us that God saves those who
are crushed in spirit. He can bring you through, he can give you strength
to keep going.

Lord, cause me to taste and see your goodness today. Amen.

TONY HORSFALL

Unanswered prayers

Contend, Lord, with those who contend with me; fight against those who fight against me. Take up shield and armour; arise and come to my aid… Then my soul will rejoice in the Lord and delight in his salvation… When my prayers returned to me unanswered, I went about mourning as though for my friend or brother. I bowed my head in grief as though weeping for my mother.

Prayer remains a great mystery to me. Who has not been baffled by the fact that sometimes our prayers are answered, and sometimes it seems they are not? David was certainly confused when his prayers were returned unanswered.

After the great deliverance described in Psalm 34, David is again embroiled in conflict with enemies on every side, false witnesses accusing him and some even seeking his life. It all felt unjust and without good reason. He did not know whom he could trust, but he did assume he could trust God. And since God had recently acted on his behalf, he assumed he would do so again. Yet in his moment of great need and despite his persistent cry for help, God is unresponsive. He feels let down.

When hopes are not fulfilled and dreams are shattered, we experience grief. Unanswered prayer is a form of loss, because it challenges our understanding of who God is and how he works. How are we to understand such times?

Prayer does not work like a slot machine, and there is no formula that guarantees God will always do what we want. Delays do not mean he is uninterested; rather, they suggest that we may be asking wrongly or that he has a greater purpose in mind, perhaps allowing us to experience trouble so that our character can be shaped and formed. God's timing may be different to ours, and his agenda may be beyond our present understanding. What is crucial is that we trust him as much in the darkness as in the light; to steadfastly hold onto him in our confusion as in our clarity.

Lord, you know my present struggles and the darkness that surrounds me. Be the light for my path and give me grace to wait patiently for you. Amen.

TONY HORSFALL

Do not be silent

How long, Lord, will you look on? Rescue me from their ravages, my precious life from these lions… Do not let those gloat over me who are my enemies without cause; do not let those who hate me without reason maliciously wink the eye… May those who delight in my vindication shout for joy and gladness; may they always say, 'The Lord be exalted, who delights in the well-being of his servant.'

It was an English clergyman, Thomas Fuller (1608–61), who coined the phrase, 'The darkest hour is just before the dawn.' This psalm does not have a happy ending, but there are glimpses of light breaking through the darkness and evidence that hope is rising within David's heart that he will come through this ordeal. Perhaps his time of waiting is drawing to a close.

The false accusations and vicious taunts continue to wound David, however, who again asserts his innocence. What troubles him most is the absence of any response from his God who appears to be silent and far away (v. 22).

Interestingly, Jesus saw a fulfilment of the words of this psalm in the rejection and hostility he experienced from the religious leaders of his day, identifying with David's experience in verse 19: 'They hated me without reason' (John 15:25). Not only did Jesus endure similar situations to us, but the fact that he knew the kind of pain that we suffer means he can understand our hurt and can help us in our time of need: 'For we do not have a high priest who is unable to feel sympathy for our weaknesses, but we have one who has been tempted in every way, just as we are – yet he did not sin' (Hebrews 4:15).

David is strengthened by the knowledge he still has some faithful friends and takes heart from his assurance that God 'delights in the well-being of his servant' (v. 27). These are two anchor points in the storms of life – for him and for all who seek to follow God in tumultuous times.

Lord, thank you for the grip of grace. Your hold on me remains firm,
even though my hold on you is sometimes weak. Amen.

TONY HORSFALL

A message from God

Your love, Lord, reaches to the heavens, your faithfulness to the skies. Your righteousness is like the highest mountains, your justice like the great deep. You, Lord, preserve both people and animals. How priceless is your unfailing love, O God! People take refuge in the shadow of your wings. They feast in the abundance of your house; you give them drink from your river of delights. For with you is the fountain of life; in your light we see light.

After the darkness of the previous psalm, this song bursts forth like a sunny summer's day with a glorious description of the wonderful character of God. How do we know what God is like? Not because we are capable of articulating it ourselves but because he has chosen to reveal himself to us through his servants, David among them. Here we see God's absolute goodness expressed in his love, faithfulness, righteousness and justice. These are abiding characteristics and will never change, because God does not change.

We see his kindness in caring for people and animals alike, and his graciousness in inviting all to find refuge in him. None are excluded and all are welcomed. We see his generosity in the way he gives abundantly to his people, providing food and drink, and satisfying both physical and spiritual needs. God is the source of all we need.

Yet David sounds a note of realism too, contrasting the faithfulness of God with the faithlessness of people. We wonder why it is, given who God is, that people turn away from him. The root cause is given in verse 1: 'There is no fear of God before their eyes.' This insight is taken up by the apostle Paul in his devastating critique of the human condition in Romans 1—3 (see 3:18 in particular). Pride and lack of respect for God cause people to go their own way, to ignore the goodness of God and to refuse to give him thanks.

Each of us must choose our own path, either towards the God who loves us with unfailing love or away from him and into the darkness of conceit and self-will.

Lord, you have set my feet on the good way. Help me to keep walking in the same direction, towards the light. Amen.

TONY HORSFALL

The Third Sunday of Lent 97

Do not fret

Do not fret because of those who are evil or be envious of those who do wrong; for like the grass they will soon wither, like green plants they will soon die away. Trust in the Lord and do good; dwell in the land and enjoy safe pasture. Take delight in the Lord, and he will give you the desires of your heart… But the meek will inherit the land and enjoy peace and prosperity.

To fret is to be constantly or visibly anxious. For David, and many believers, a cause of anxiety is to see that wicked people often seem to prosper while good people often suffer. This seems unjust and unfair. Why does God allow it?

This psalm is in the tradition of wisdom literature, like the book of Proverbs. It contains a series of short statements, mostly expressing a contrast between the righteous and the wicked and extolling the value of a life that is centred on God and seeks to honour him in every way. Such a way of living will know God's blessing and ultimately be seen to be the better way to live.

Commentators suggest that verse 11 was the inspiration behind the third beatitude: 'Blessed are the meek, for they will inherit the earth' (Matthew 5:5). In the kingdom that Jesus inaugurated it is the humble and self-effacing who are valued, not those who are pushy and self-promoting. They may not get on in this life, but their faith assures those who are meek (gentle and lowly of heart) of blessing in the life to come.

Such a lifestyle is countercultural and radical, yet meekness is not weakness. Only strong people can choose to swim against the tide, to live with honesty and integrity, even if by doing so they are disadvantaged. The meek are those whose trust is in God, who find delight in knowing him and who commit their way to him. They have no need to be jealous of others who gain temporary success or prosperity. The smile of God's approval is sufficient for them; with that they are content.

Lord, forgive me for allowing the strivings of the world to infect my heart. Help me rest content in the joy of knowing you. Amen.

TONY HORSFALL

Under the Lord's care

I was young and now I am old, yet I have never seen the righteous forsaken or their children begging bread. They are always generous and lend freely; their children will be a blessing. Turn from evil and do good; then you will dwell in the land forever. For the Lord loves the just and will not forsake his faithful ones… Hope in the Lord and keep his way.

The second half of the psalm continues to draw out the sobering contrast between two approaches to life – the wicked wilfully turning away from God to a chosen separation from him; the righteous turning towards God and a life lived under his care.

In the midst of it all we find this beautiful testimony to a life well lived as one of the 'meek', the story of someone who has been quietly faithful to God through all the ups and downs of life.

I wonder what lies between the statements 'I was young' and 'now I am old'? Probably decades of following God steadily, albeit imperfectly at times, and years of seeking to do his will no matter what the cost. Happy days, sad days and many humdrum days. A tapestry of memories both good and bad – celebration and disappointment, joy and sorrow. And now the contentment of old age and a glad awareness of still being 'under the Lord's care' (v. 18).

How would you reflect on the days of your life? What have been the highlights? What have been the low points? What have you discovered about God? What have you learned about yourself? What is your testimony?

I love the picture of family life that emerges from these verses, even though it may be idealised. Here is a family unit that has known God's daily provision, whether in plenty or just enough. There has been a conscious awareness of God in their life together, and his generosity towards them has made them generous towards others. Kindness has recreated kindness, and young people who have grown up in an atmosphere of blessing in turn become a blessing to others in adulthood.

Lord, today I ask your blessing on my own family, and other families that come to mind as I pause. Amen.

TONY HORSFALL

My sinful folly

Lord, do not rebuke me in your anger or discipline me in your wrath. Your arrows have pierced me, and your hand has come down on me. Because of your wrath there is no health in my body; there is no soundness in my bones because of my sin… Lord, do not forsake me; do not be far from me, my God. Come quickly to help me, my Lord and my Saviour.

This can only be described as a sad psalm, the cry of a believer who is suffering greatly. Its importance lies in the connection made between sin and suffering.

The unpalatable truth is that God sometimes disciplines us to wean us from our sinful ways. He allows suffering to come into our lives as a wake-up call, a reminder that sin always has consequences. David is very clear that he has sinned (v. 3), that his suffering is because of his sinful folly (v. 5) and that his conscience is deeply troubled as a result (v. 18). He is also sure that his dis-ease (physical pain and emotional anguish) is a consequence of his breaking God's laws. He does not regard his suffering as unjust; it is restorative, the chastening hand of a God who loves him.

At the same time, we must be clear that not all suffering is the result of sin. Nor is it always a discipline from God. We cannot make a judgement about another's pain. Only the individual knows what has taken place, and they alone can say if God is disciplining them. They will know because they are aware of specific sin, and their conscience is genuinely troubled.

Even in this moment of failure David is aware of God's presence and grace. God is dealing with him (v. 1), and nothing is hidden from his sight (v. 9). He knows that God will respond, and he is learning to wait (v. 15). Even now, God will not forsake him and will eventually help him (vv. 21–22). This is the joy of the gospel – we are never too far gone for God to save us.

Lord, help me to keep a watch on my life; save me from my own folly.
Thank you that discipline is an expression of your love. Amen.

TONY HORSFALL

The brevity of life

'Show me, Lord, my life's end and the number of my days; let me know how fleeting my life is. You have made my days a mere handbreadth; the span of my years is as nothing before you. Everyone is but a breath, even those who seem secure. Surely everyone goes around like a mere phantom; in vain they rush about, heaping up wealth without knowing whose it will finally be. But now, Lord, what do I look for? My hope is in you.'

I read an amusing article about how different people signed off their letters. Apparently, an undertaker ended his with the phrase, 'Yours, eventually.'

There is an obvious continuation of thought here from David's musings in Psalm 38. Now he is angry with God because of the severity of the treatment he has received but chooses not to vent his feelings lest he gives God a bad name. At the same time, he has learnt a vital lesson from his suffering – that life is short and to be appreciated.

David's melancholic mood echoes that of the writer of Ecclesiastes, yet there is wisdom here, especially for our present times. We must not take life for granted but treasure each moment as a gift and make the most of it, for it can end more quickly than we realise. We may have good health care, follow a heathy diet and keep ourselves fit, yet life is still fragile. Furthermore, even if we enjoy long life, when we look back, it will seem to have gone in a flash.

Busyness helps many to keep such troubling thoughts at bay. It is characteristic of 21st-century life that people are always rushing in a relentless pursuit of money and material comforts. With no time to think and no inclination to reflect on the fleeting nature of life, we protect ourselves against the sobering thought that one day our lives will end.

Even though he is upset with God, David knows his only hope is to trust in him. Nothing in this earthly life can give lasting peace or satisfaction. Eternity beckons, and we must be ready and prepared for the life to come.

Lord, these are unsettling thoughts, but necessary. Let me be ready when you call me home. Amen.

TONY HORSFALL

Here I am

'I waited patiently for the Lord; he turned to me and heard my cry… Sacrifice and offering you did not desire – but my ears you have opened; – burnt offerings and sin offerings you did not require. Then I said, 'Here I am, I have come – it is written about me in the scroll. I desire to do your will, my God; your law is within my heart.'

David's celebration of his deliverance is best seen in the context of the two preceding psalms, where the call to wait patiently and to trust were seen as the only way through. Now God has acted, and David's feet are secure again. Inevitably, his joy is expressed in song and his life becomes a message of hope to others. His deepest response, however, is to offer himself fully to God and to do his will, an offering of much greater value than any animal sacrifice.

These words (vv. 6–8) find their fulfilment in Jesus and the writer to the Hebrews explains their significance more fully (Hebrews 10:5–10). Jesus came into the world to do his Father's will, to fulfil the law and offer himself as the lamb of God as a once-for-all-time sacrifice for the sin of the world. This has two implications. First, the old system of animal sacrifice is now obsolete, since Christ's sacrifice is perfect and sufficient to remove sin permanently and completely. It does not need to be repeated. Second, all who trust in him are made acceptable to God (holy) through this offering of himself. No other sacrifice is needed. He is able to lift us from the mess of sin and set our feet on solid ground, forgiven, cleansed and restored.

And what is our response to such an amazing truth? It is to offer ourselves to him, to surrender to his love and to seek to do his will. We can do this without fear, since he only wants the best for us, and we can entrust him with our lives.

Make this your prayer today: 'Were the whole realm of nature mine, that were an offering far too small. Love so amazing, so divine, demands my soul, my life, my all' (Isaac Watts, 1674–1748). Amen.

TONY HORSFALL

Testimony

I proclaim your saving acts in the great assembly; I do not seal my lips, Lord, as you know. I do not hide your righteousness in my heart; I speak of your faithfulness and your saving help. I do not conceal your love and faithfulness from the great assembly... But as for me, I am poor and needy; may the Lord think of me. You are my help and my deliverer; you are my God, do not delay.

David had a ready-made outlet for his thanksgiving to God – he could sing and play music, so psalms were his natural expression. We appreciate worship leaders and songwriters who craft beautiful lyrics and compose memorable tunes to enhance our worship, but the majority of us could never aspire to this. How can we share our experience of God?

We can do so by sharing our testimony, telling the story of what God has done for us. If we are shy or introverted, we may baulk at the thought of speaking publicly. Maybe we could share in a more intimate setting, like a home group or over coffee with a close friend. Alternatively, we could write something for the church magazine. What we do not want is to 'seal our lips' and prevent others from having the opportunity to hear what God has done.

Others may be more comfortable to speak in a congregational setting, talking freely about God's faithfulness. Not only does this strengthen the person who testifies, but it also glorifies God and gives others the opportunity to learn more about God. A personal anecdote about the power of God at work in our lives is a good way to share with those who are not yet believers. Everyone likes a good story, and personal experience has high value.

David, however, is not living on a 'high'. He is still surrounded by troubles, struggling with sin (v. 12) and taunted by his enemies (vv. 14–15). His realism causes him to cry again to God for help. He has experienced an amazing deliverance, but he remains poor and needy – as do we all.

Lord, give me greater boldness in speaking of your goodness,
and the humility to daily depend on you. Amen.

TONY HORSFALL

If you've enjoyed this set of reflections by **Tony Horsfall**,
check out his books published with BRF Ministries, including…

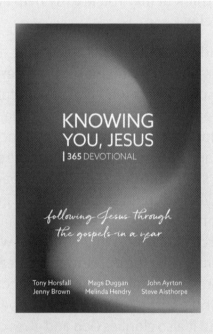

Knowing You, Jesus
*Following Jesus through
the gospels in a year*

978 1 80039 185 7
£19.99

To order, visit **brfonline.org.uk** or use the order form at the end.

Lamentations

Lament is a passionate expression of grief or sorrow. It is marked by deep longing and an intensity because of its effect on those who suffer. Although it is possible to lament for many situations, the word is most often associated with a religious life. In these readings we will see the depth of the grief experienced by the prophet whom many believe was Jeremiah. What has occasioned his poetry is not in doubt: the nation has been taken captive and removed to Babylon.

The exile is often regarded as the most profound national trauma the Hebrews experienced in biblical times. It shook their faith in God to the core, because it appeared to signal God had forgotten his people, that his promises had failed and covenants been revoked. This shattering experience was intensified because, apart from the land, it was not possible to worship God and serve him. One of the most fruitful discoveries in this period however (in the writings of Ezekiel, for example) was that God could indeed be encountered elsewhere and that his power extended over all the earth.

This book is a set of poems woven together very carefully. They wrestle with the causes of Judah's destruction, the role played by leaders and how enemies have triumphed despite their own wickedness. However, it sets these physical questions within much deeper ones about God and his purposes. The prophet places the steadfast love of the Lord at the heart of his preaching because he is quite sure God does not change but needs to work through the implications of this and what it means for the people.

This is an exceptional book, because it demands answers which are not easy to articulate and less easy still to contemplate. But lamentation is a proper response to situations which go wrong and where wrong is done and a response is essential. The writings possess a realism sometimes lacking in our discourse both in the nation and church and invite us to reflect again on our own responsibility to be faithful.

I hope and pray they inspire you to a deeper sense of God's own lament for us and for the world and to join in his work of the coming of the kingdom.

ANDY JOHN

Jerusalem in ruins

How lonely sits the city that once was full of people! How like a widow she has become, she that was great among the nations! She that was a princess among the provinces has become subject to forced labour. She weeps bitterly in the night, with tears on her cheeks; among all her lovers, she has no one to comfort her; all her friends have dealt treacherously with her; they have become her enemies.

It is difficult for us to understand how traumatic the exile was in 597BC for God's people. Their identity had been grounded on several founding gifts: the promise of a homeland, the covenants, the gift of the law and the work of the prophets. These 'guaranteed' an ongoing relationship with God, in which there was divine grace and human accountability. Throughout Israel's history there were shock moments when a re-evaluation of their commitment was necessary (such as in the eighth century BC), but there was no wholescale collapse of national and religious life and no destruction which appeared to end everything upon which life had been built. This all changed with their captivity in Babylon, when God appeared to have finally abandoned them to their fate.

Our reading today paints a vivid picture of Jerusalem's destruction. Where once she enjoyed commerce and prosperity, now there is poverty and ruin. There is no one to assist or comfort her. Like a widow locked inside her grief, she can only lament bitterly that her situation is beyond all human help.

Although this experience was desperate for God's people, it did evoke a deeper reflection on the way God's gifts were to be received and ultimately who God was. From within this new thinking, fresh perspectives emerged on what faithful living involved and the kind of trust which can survive moments of uncertainty and hardship. It will be true for us too that decisive moments come which require us to reorient our lives. Whether we have been like the prodigal in Jesus' story (Luke 15:11–32) or have simply experienced a personal trauma, the upheaval presents an opportunity to lean on God, to re-evaluate and to address our situation with new faith.

Almighty God, deliver us from things which hold us captive,
and make us your own. For Christ's sake. Amen.

ANDY JOHN

Jeremiah's agony

Is it nothing to you, all you who pass by? Look and see if there is any sorrow like my sorrow, which was brought upon me, which the Lord inflicted on the day of his fierce anger. From on high he sent fire; it went deep into my bones; he spread a net for my feet; he turned me back; he has left me stunned, faint all day long.

We may be familiar with these words. Good Friday services occasionally include them as a way of describing the sorrows Jesus experienced. They capture the prophet's lament as he weeps for the city of Jerusalem. What is dramatic here is that the prophet makes the city and nation's grief his own. He becomes one with the land so that the sorrow of the whole nation is also his own sorrow. The punishment he endures is in fact visited upon everyone. In this way the experience reads with greater intensity.

Collective trauma is one of the most challenging dynamics known to us. Those involved in the healing of Rwanda following the genocide of the 1990s know how deeply rooted suspicions and mistrust can be. And these are matched by levels of anxiety which do not heal easily. However, the work of reconciliation brings an opportunity to reassess assumptions. This will involve patient listening to the experiences of others and becoming attentive to voices that are different from our own. But it will also necessitate acknowledging the scale and consequences of our own wrongdoing. We come face to face with awkward truths about ourselves, and this can be sobering. It is also necessary before any realignment to the good purposes of God can take place.

In this sense, even the trauma described here presents an opportunity. A healed and restored people can show signs of redeeming love, the power of forgiveness and the hope of a future beyond the present. And this, of course, is true for us today as much as for the land in 597BC.

Living God, in the desolation of sin we see the reality of our wrongdoing and of the world. Give us honesty and the courage to face the truth, that we may be healed. Amen.

ANDY JOHN

The Lord punishes

The Lord has become like an enemy; he has destroyed Israel. He has destroyed all its palaces, laid in ruins its strongholds, and multiplied in daughter Judah mourning and lamentation. He has broken down his booth like a garden; he has destroyed his tabernacle; the Lord has abolished in Zion festival and Sabbath and in his fierce indignation has spurned king and priest. The Lord has scorned his altar, disowned his sanctuary; he has delivered into the hand of the enemy the walls of her palaces.

In our reading today the prophet describes the terror of realising God has become 'the enemy'. In an astonishing piece of writing, he describes God as the very one who does what other nations had previously done. This association is easily lost but needs unpacking. At one level, this is not completely new, because everything – even chastisement – occurs within the permissive will of God. But to take the next step and associate God directly with one's enemies is remarkable.

The prophet's experience of God leads to this conclusion, and it would be too easy to dismiss this as an emotional response on his part. We might be familiar with C.S. Lewis' bold statement from *The Lion, the Witch and the Wardrobe* that 'Aslan is not a tame lion'. Lucy also asks whether Aslan is safe. Mr Beaver gets to the point: 'Safe? Who said anything about being safe. 'Course he isn't safe. But he's good. He's the King, I tell you.'

The nation experienced not a different God who punished their sin, but the very God who had given so much. In the gift there comes a necessary response of faithfulness which Paul described as the obedience of faith (Romans 1:5). In truth, it is very easy to make God in our own image and justify our actions with reference to God. Countless nations, communities, churches and individuals have done this very thing – and, of course, it is monstrous.

Our task as Christians is to hear the word of lamentation afresh and understand that our actions do have repercussions. There can be no true grace without true holiness, and this alone makes for a closer walk with God.

Heavenly Father, teach us to align our lives to your good and perfect will and to long for the things of your kingdom. For Jesus Christ's sake. Amen.

ANDY JOHN

New perspectives

The steadfast love of the Lord never ceases, his mercies never come to an end; they are new every morning; great is your faithfulness. 'The Lord is my portion,' says my soul, 'therefore I will hope in him.' The Lord is good to those who wait for him, to the soul that seeks him. It is good that one should wait quietly for the salvation of the Lord.

The words in our reading today are some of the most beautiful and best known in the Old Testament. Many hymns and choruses have been written to include them. What makes them remarkable is their context. We have heard that the city is in ruins, desolate, and that the land is broken and its people taken captive. The circumstances do not invite this kind of faithful affirmation, but this is the very nature of faith. When God called Abram, he promised he would make of him a great nation (Genesis 12:2). Abram was 75 years old and had little upon which to base his confident departure other than believing God.

Statements of faith like this are life-changing. They allow us to set our circumstances within a context of divine grace. God is not outside of the picture but present with us calling us forward. This in turn changes our perception of those realities we had thought were only dark and foreboding and in which God seemed absent. They might not offer the clarity we hope for, but they provide the kind of base from which to live faithfully whatever we face.

As a cleric, I have experienced those who are nearing the time of their death and who repeatedly draw on God's help for strength and peace. Disciples of Jesus know that death is not the end. So when our bodies fail us, there is the face-to-face with God awaiting and this is the most precious thing we possess. It is here, at the big moments, when we need most of all to hear the enduring word which tells us the steadfast love of the Lord never ceases, his mercies never come to an end.

Merciful God, your love endures all things even to the end.
May this love consume in us all that is wrong and hold us fast each day.
For Jesus' sake. Amen.

ANDY JOHN

Hunted like a bird

Those who were my enemies without cause have hunted me like a bird; they flung me alive into a pit and hurled stones on me; water closed over my head; I said, 'I am lost.' I called on your name, O Lord, from the depths of the pit; you heard my plea, 'Do not close your ear to my cry for help, but give me relief!' You came near when I called on you; you said, 'Do not fear!'

It would be tempting to imagine our book would end with verses from yesterday's reading. It would be neat and tidy. Life is seldom like this, and the repeating circles of lament we read today have a realism about them. We have seen that the prophet has personified Jerusalem and the whole nation with himself. What he experiences is the same as the whole land. But he returns to his complaint in order to take up his cause with God. Enemies have unjustly attacked, tortured and abused him. In desperation he cries out to God.

This is one of the most difficult aspects of faith with which to grapple: why does a loving God allow suffering and injustice? As we view our world with its numerous wars, we could conclude at one level that most suffering is caused by human beings. God is often blamed for our own failures. But this will not satisfy those who suffer innocently, either through ill health or circumstances beyond their control. The great tsunami on Boxing Day 2004 killed an estimated 227,898 people, none of whom 'deserved' to die.

Our world is not perfect. Injustices flourish unchecked, and many die without any to help them. Perhaps it is hard to conceive of a world that is perfect and where everything is in balance, but I believe that when we pray for the kingdom to come, we are praying for the hastening of that time. We are urging God and seeking ourselves to stand at his side for things to be different. And this prayer therefore invites us to participate in the transformation of all of life. We might lament because of our broken world, but we are not powerless to change it. Neither is the almighty God.

Lord, teach us to wrestle with you as we pray, and may your kingdom of justice come soon, for we ask this in his name, Jesus Christ our Lord. Amen.

ANDY JOHN

The failure of faith

It was for the sins of her prophets and the iniquities of her priests, who shed the blood of the righteous in her midst. Blindly they wandered through the streets, so defiled with blood that no one was able to touch their garments. 'Away! Unclean!' people shouted at them; 'Away! Away! Do not touch!' So they became fugitives and wanderers; it was said among the nations, 'They shall stay here no longer.'

Corruption is endemic in many parts of our world. It affects industry, politics and the religious institutions which are often the backbone of communal life. When this kind of failure extends to those who are called to lead, a community cannot flourish and is likely to collapse in due course.

This is the accusation made against the prophets and priests, from whom we should expect the highest of standards. In their time, the religious framework extended to every part of life. Devotion to God was therefore clearly marked; infractions were serious matters often leading to censure and an appropriate response. It was the priests who oversaw faithfulness to the law and the rituals of sacrifice and the prophets who spoke God's immediate word. These would have been significant figures, the 'holy' ones devoted to God in a special way. But their corruption has infected them so entirely that they have become the very thing they were called to protect. Now defiled, they are driven away because of their uncleanness.

It is common to hear today of the call for high standards in public life, and this is necessary. But in my experience, it is impossible to maintain this without an ordered private life. If chaos characterises an inner life, it is difficult to see how this will not break out into the public arena. Leaders cannot model what they do not possess themselves. There is a clear warning here for everyone called to oversight in any sphere. We do well to remember Jesus' words regarding hypocrisy (Matthew 7:3–5) and the double standards this involves.

Faithful God, you give us standards which protect and enable good society to flourish and the church to grow. May our leaders live their calling according to your ways. In Jesus Christ's name. Amen.

ANDY JOHN

What of our future?

But you, O Lord, reign forever; your throne endures to all generations. Why have you forgotten us completely? Why have you forsaken us these many days? Restore us to yourself, O Lord, that we may be restored; renew our days as of old – unless you have utterly rejected us and are angry with us beyond measure.

Our final reading holds in tension themes we have been exploring in these poems. The affirmation of faith in God and his enduring reign is followed by a pitiful cry, a plea that the future might not be permanent abandonment. When we recall the reality of the exile, these two seemingly contradictory statements do not seem so far apart.

My favourite Advent hymn is the beautiful prayer, 1,200 years old, which originated in monastery life and was modernised by John Mason Neale (1818–66) and sung to the tune 'Veni Emmanuel'. 'O come, O come, Emmanuel' uses this same tension to invite deeper praying. The Old Testament exile provides a picture for our own understanding of the present age, for although we are citizens of heaven, we yearn for the coming age when God will be king. In the words of Paul, now 'we see only a reflection, as in a mirror, but then we will see face to face' (1 Corinthians 13:12).

In the exile this tension is so great that it must have felt at breaking point. God is Lord of all and cannot be less than God. And yet the faithful languished in exile and felt far from him. Very often we hold these kinds of tension together in our own lives. We know God to be kind and good, but our circumstances are troubling. Sometimes we need others to hold these two things together with us so that we are not overwhelmed by our situation. The light of God does come, but the waiting can be the hardest part.

I want to end these readings with a prayer if this is you: Great and loving God, when we feel desperate and abandoned, give us a faith that sees beyond our situation. Send your Holy Spirit to comfort us and bring us safely to the place of safety. For Jesus Christ's sake. Amen.

ANDY JOHN

The passion according to John

John 18—19 are surely two of the richest chapters in what is, in many ways, the richest of all the gospels. And having the temerity to pass any comment on them certainly feels like rushing – or rather tiptoeing – in where angels fear to tread.

Re-reading them, I am struck again by the tangled web that is good and evil. Annas and Caiaphas – priestly or self-serving? Peter – lion or chicken? Pilate – cynical or doubtful? Jesus – victim or agent? We surely know, for ourselves as well as for the cast in this seemingly final act of Jesus' life on earth, that it is not a case of either-or, but both-and. Change our circumstances, and who knows what hitherto hidden facets of our character may emerge. We are all, indeed, multifaceted.

There is another conundrum: the oft-quoted saying, attributed to Edmund Burke (1729–97), that 'all that is necessary for evil to triumph is for good men to do nothing' appears to be turned on its head here. It seems that, on the contrary, in order for the will of God finally to triumph, the well-meaning attempts of 'good' men must come to nothing. Really? It would be nice if the chain of cause and effect, the consequences of right and wrong, were more straightforward, but life is more complicated. It is a tangled web indeed, in the face of which our best response may often be not to seek to understand, but to trust that indeed God is at work in all things, for our good. Remember the parable of the wheat and the weeds? It is only finally that all will be untangled – to mix the metaphors – by the master weaver.

One newspaper I read has a section on 'heroes and villains', but, oh, it is so *not* like that! Yes, an *action* may be heroic or villainous, but that does not define us; we remain as complex as ever, capable of we know not what in different times and seasons. Yet with Jesus and with God there is a bigger story. May these reflections offer something of a corrective in our dualistic, in-out, black-white, blame-seeking culture, and remind us all of the need for humility and compassion – and hope.

SHEILA WALKER

Stage manager

Then Jesus, knowing all that was to happen to him, came forward and asked them, 'Whom are you looking for?' They answered, 'Jesus of Nazareth.' Jesus replied, 'I am he.' Judas, who betrayed him, was standing with them. When Jesus said to them, 'I am he,' they stepped back and fell to the ground. Again he asked them, 'Whom are you looking for?' And they said, 'Jesus of Nazareth.'

Gethsemane. Away from the crowds and busyness of Jerusalem at Passover. After dark. Easier, then, for the temple police and the Roman soldiers to make an arrest. Less chance of a skirmish, of that maverick's followers coming to his aid. Not that they are taking any chances, there must be dozens of them, with their torches and weapons.

Yet whose decision is it to come here? Surely not theirs. It is Jesus who leads his disciples here; Jesus who, after hours spent agonising in prayer to his Father, knows all that is to happen to him; and Jesus who takes the initiative and goes forward to meet the soldiers. It is his choice for there not to be a battle, for there to be no loss of life among his disciples or other followers. What lies ahead is for him alone. He sets the scene: he is the stage manager.

It is significant that, as he confesses 'I am', his accusers fall to the ground. These are surely no mere words of identification, but imbued with all the significance of the sacred name of God revealed to Moses (Exodus 3:14). In this darkest of all nights there comes, as it were, a sudden flash of lightning, a reminder of what can still, in theory, be possible: a summoning of legions of angels to rescue Jesus from the excruciating hours ahead. But no. That is not part of the divine plot.

The stage is set, and the drama must be enacted as written. This is not so much an arrest as a surrender on the part of Jesus. His death is not forced upon him but accepted and met willingly, albeit after a very human inner struggle. What greater evidence of the love of God is there for us?

Gracious God, when it seems that all around evil is triumphing,
may we remember that you are sovereign, and the final act will celebrate
your victory. Amen.

SHEILA WALKER

Scapegoat

So the soldiers, their officer, and the Jewish police arrested Jesus and bound him. First they took him to Annas, who was the father-in-law of Caiaphas, the high priest that year. Caiaphas was the one who had advised the Jews that it was better to have one person die for the people.

Why Annas? Though high priest from AD6–15, he is now technically 'retired', having been deposed by the previous Roman procurator. It is perhaps an indication of the tension among the authorities and their concern that timing is of the essence that they first call in the big guns, as it were, seeking the wisdom of age and experience. Or perhaps it is Annas himself who 'pulls rank' and insists on seeing Jesus first and immediately, even though it is the middle of the night.

It is not Annas, however, but his son-in-law Caiaphas who has spoken prophetically. Following Jesus' raising of Lazarus from the dead, many more are coming to believe in him, and the priests and the Pharisees are worried. If he gains too great a following, surely it will alarm the Roman authorities, who will then crack down on all things Jewish. To Caiaphas, though, this is a no-brainer. One man's life is surely a small price to pay if it secures the well-being of many. Blame Jesus, dig the dirt, stitch him up, job done.

Scapegoating. We may not call it that today, but it is as prevalent as ever. Who is to blame for what goes wrong? There must surely be someone, a name; it cannot be all of us, that would be just too hard to deal with. Maybe it is our ancestors, whose reputations, along with their statues, must be toppled. Maybe it is the industry boss who failed to spot a fraudulent employee. Maybe it is the politician who got drunk and behaved inappropriately. Fault is found. Heads must roll. Many a talent has perhaps been sacrificed on the altar of proxy absolution. As if the rest of us were perfect!

Lord, it is only when we acknowledge our own imperfection that we are able to be amazed and thankful that Caiaphas spoke more truly than he knew. May knowledge of your forgiveness take the place of any need to blame in my life. Amen.

SHEILA WALKER

Alone

Simon Peter and another disciple followed Jesus. Since that disciple was known to the high priest, he went with Jesus into the courtyard… but Peter was standing outside at the gate. So the other disciple… spoke to the woman who guarded the gate, and brought Peter in. The woman said to Peter, 'You are not also one of this man's disciples, are you?' He said, 'I am not.' Now, the slaves and the police had made a charcoal fire because it was cold, and they were standing around it and warming themselves. Peter also was standing with them and warming himself.

It is easy to to condemn Peter for his disloyalty. How *could* he? Only a few moments ago he was drawing his sword, albeit mistakenly, to defend Jesus. But perhaps that is part of the problem. Why does Jesus not want to put up any kind of a fight? For heaven's sake, he is seeming almost to welcome his own arrest! To want to go it alone! What is going on?

We can appreciate something of the confusion now clouding Peter's brain: the events of this night are challenging his understanding of the Jesus he knows and loves. Despite Jesus' warnings, Peter still cannot accept that the Messiah is to be arrested and killed. Is he then the Messiah? Was I wrong to hail him as such? Was he wrong to accept the title?

Remember that it is still the middle of the night. We all know how diso-riented we feel when woken suddenly in the early hours; it is rarely the best time to make decisions. While the cold may have an invigorating effect, maybe the warmth of the fire is making him drowsy again. For the second time that night, sheer human tiredness scuppers his need for watchfulness.

It also is the way the woman phrases the question: you are *not* one of this man's disciples? This anticipates the answer 'No.' How easy it is for us, almost automatically, to give people the answer they expect: easier than to upset, to challenge, and maybe then to be challenged in return, especially when we are not sure we have our defence in place.

Lord, while none of this excuses Peter's denial, it surely stands as a salutary reminder of our own frailty and perhaps failure to be ready to confess Christ in the public arena. Please forgive me, grant me clear thinking and the courage not to disappoint you. Amen.

SHEILA WALKER

Sincere

Then the high priest questioned Jesus about his disciples and about his teaching. Jesus answered, 'I have spoken openly to the world; I have always taught in synagogues and in the temple, where all the Jews come together. I have said nothing in secret. Why do you ask me? Ask those who heard what I said to them; they know what I said.'

My favourite understanding of the word 'sincere' – apparently now discredited by some experts – is that it derives from the Latin *sine* (without) and *cera* (wax). This goes back to the time when Renaissance sculptors would cover any defects in their work with wax. When exposed to sunlight, however, the wax would melt and the faults would be exposed. Those sculptures without any wax therefore became known as *sincera*: without wax, whole, unadulterated, pure.

Thus Jesus is able to say of his teaching: 'Go on, inspect it; ask anyone. There is nothing secret, no dissimulation, nothing I would ever wish to apologise for, qualify or conceal.' He has been first to the synagogues in each place: the Jewish leaders and priests can testify to his words. He has shared parables with the crowds, performed miracles and healed openly: the general public can testify to all of this. He has given further teaching to those closest to him: the disciples can vouch for all he has said. In the trial that is to come, there is to be no selection or manipulation of evidence to make the best case, no searching for legal loopholes, no attempt at mitigation of any kind. Jesus' teaching is what it is. Jesus is who he is. The outcome will be what it will be.

I wonder how many of us – if any! – can say the same. No words we wish we could bite back. No emails we wish we had never sent. No gossip, insensitive remark, half-truth. And hardest of all, those thoughts which betray all too painfully that there is still all too much of the 'old' being to be dealt with, all too many defects still, whether or not we try to apply some kind of wax to conceal them.

Come, Lord, with your refiner's fire and purify us, so that others may be able to see your image reflected in every part of our lives. Amen.

SHEILA WALKER

Foreseeing

Now Simon Peter was standing and warming himself. They asked him, 'You are not also one of his disciples, are you?' He denied it and said, 'I am not.' One of the slaves of the high priest, a relative of the man whose ear Peter had cut off, asked, 'Did I not see you in the garden with him?' Again Peter denied it, and at that moment the cock crowed.

How true that the spirit is willing, but the flesh is weak! It is only a matter of hours since Peter has declared that he is prepared to die for Jesus, only for Jesus to tell him of his threefold denial before the cock crows. Is Peter not listening? Possibly not, given the emotion of the moment. Does he simply discount the warning? Possibly, given his impetuous, generous nature. Or does it come back to the age-old conundrum: if something is prophesied, is its fulfilment inevitable? If Jesus, in this instance, has said it will happen, could Peter have acted any differently?

Imagine, for a moment, what would have happened had Peter admitted he was with Jesus. Would it have spelled imprisonment for him? Death? What then of the years of amazing apostolic ministry which we know lay ahead of him? True, he will indeed die for his loyalty to Jesus, but not yet. Is it possible to say that, somehow or other, God is at work even in this seemingly cowardly and unforgivable denial – at work for good?

There is hardly the space for complex theological or philosophical debate, which I suspect would in any case bring us back to the challenge of living with paradox. It is perhaps an encouragement for us to know that none of our failures will finally thwart the will of God or outweigh his ability and willingness to forgive and restore (John 21: 15–19). If failure awakens us to our need to renounce our self-sufficiency and, as the energy companies would have it, 'switch providers' to the power of the Holy Spirit, can even failure then be a tool in the hand of God?

Gracious God, thank you that our failings are already factored into your plans; all that we are is known to you and all is redeemable. Praise be! Amen.

SHEILA WALKER

Regal

Then Pilate entered the headquarters again, summoned Jesus, and asked him, 'Are you the King of the Jews?' Jesus answered, 'Do you ask this on your own, or did others tell you about me?' Pilate replied, 'I am not a Jew, am I? Your own nation and the chief priests have handed you over to me. What have you done?' Jesus answered, 'My kingdom does not belong to this world.'

John omits any account of Jesus before the Jewish supreme court, when he refuses to defend himself in the face of false witnesses but, under oath, admits to the title of Messiah, the heavenly Son of Man foretold by the prophet Daniel. This the court calls out as blasphemy, and dispatches Jesus to Pilate for the death sentence they are not permitted to carry out themselves. Perhaps they might have him quietly finished off in a back street, but a public crucifixion – seen as a mark of God's curse – will be far more effective in quelling any potential rebellion and dispersing his followers.

Is there any proof of rebellion? Does Jesus constitute a threat to Caesar, to Rome? Is he a rival king? Yes – and no, not in the sense that Pilate expects. Certainly his conduct before Pilate, and in the hours that will follow, is regal: not in the sense of flaunting authority but of demonstrating the poise of one who has nothing to prove. Jesus is neither a political nor a military figure, but his kingship is far from being mere tokenism or ceremony. Under him, royalty is reinvented; kingship is not imposed but attributed by those who choose to trust and obey. There are no geographical borders, no age, ethnicity or language requirements, simply our confession of allegiance to this king above all others.

And what does that feel like and look like to others? How does the kingship of Jesus affect my life, your life, day by day? Is the kingdom of heaven visible or invisible? Tangible or intangible? Present or still to come?

Lord, the answer to that last question is probably yes, and yes!
But I long that your kingdom may become more visible, more tangible,
more present in and through me, day by day, by your grace, through your
Spirit and for your glory. Amen.

SHEILA WALKER

Truth

Pilate asked him, 'So you are a king?' Jesus answered, 'You say that I am a king. For this I was born, and for this I came into the world, to testify to the truth. Everyone who belongs to the truth listens to my voice.' Pilate asked him, 'What is truth?'

It is hard to know *how* Pilate's question about truth is spoken. Is this a mere cynical aside or a momentary check, a challenge, a truly deep questioning? Either way, again there is neither the time nor the space for philosophical discussion; the moment passes. We too can so easily be distracted by the immediate, the urgent, from giving time to tackle the really important questions.

What is truth? We live in an age and culture which challenge any idea of absolute truth; even in science, it has been said, there are no universal truths, just views of the world that have yet to be shown to be false. It becomes hard therefore to defend any one position without being accused of being bigoted, reactionary, exclusive.

People say that what is true for you is not necessarily true for me. Why should I look to any authority other than my own feelings, judgments, traditions? Yet even Nietzsche declared, 'If God is dead, everything is permitted,' and that is exactly where much of the western world now finds itself: adrift in a somewhat anarchic sea without a compass.

'Truth' encompasses not only factual accuracy about the real world, but the question of how we should live in it. Are there such things as right and wrong? If so, is 'the greatest happiness of the greatest number' a sufficient basis? Or does morality need to transcend this? Can morality therefore derive only from the character of God, seeking to be reflected in those who are created in his image, and supremely in his own incarnate Son, Jesus Christ, who says not only that he is 'the way' and 'the life', but also 'the truth' (John 14:6)? He is not only the one whose teaching about the world is true, but also the one who embodies a godly response which is to be our inspiration and, through the power of his Holy Spirit, our enabling.

Lord, may your Spirit lead us into all truth:
in believing, and in living, day by day. Amen.

SHEILA WALKER

Sidelined

After he had said this, he went out to the Jews again and told them, 'I find no case against him. But you have a custom that I release someone for you at the Passover. Do you want me to release for you the King of the Jews?' They shouted in reply, 'Not this man but Barabbas!' Now Barabbas was a rebel.

Here we see again the tortuous interweaving of good and evil, mixed motives and the sovereignty of God at work in the midst of the maelstrom of human choices. Pilate declares that he finds no case against Jesus. That could have been the end of the story but, out of some divine or human prompting, he goes one step further, offering to release Jesus. Magnanimity or scheming?

From Pilate's point of view, that would have the advantage of easing his own conscience while implying that Jesus is indeed a criminal, and it would also be giving the people a chance for their voice to be heard over against that of the priests who are responsible for Jesus' arrest. Unfortunately, though, his plan backfires; the people are more enthusiastic about freeing Barabbas, who will help in their struggle against the occupying Romans.

When I saw the Oberammergau passion play, I noticed yellow-robed priests moving purposefully among the crowd, evidently urging people to shout for Barabbas. This may well have been the case, but in any event it is the true criminal who goes free.

With hindsight, we know that Jesus' crucifixion is an inevitable part of the divine plan. The wages of sin is death (Romans 6:23), but Jesus bears our sins in his body on the cross (1 Peter 2:24). To be crucified is regarded as being under a curse, and Jesus endures for us the curse of the law and our failure to keep it. Is it then right to say that Pilate's scheme backfires? From his point of view, perhaps. In the short term, perhaps. Humanly speaking, perhaps. But in the providential love of God, that is not the end of the story.

Lord, you do indeed write straight with our crooked lines.
May we take courage and hope from the fact that the end of every story will
reveal your grace, wisdom and love. Amen.

SHEILA WALKER

Unique

So Jesus came out wearing the crown of thorns and the purple robe. Pilate said to them, 'Behold the man!' When the chief priests and the police saw him, they shouted, 'Crucify him! Crucify him!' Pilate said to them, 'Take him yourselves and crucify him; I find no case against him.' The Jews answered him, 'We have a law, and according to that law he ought to die because he has claimed to be the Son of God.'

In an attempt to placate the crowd, Pilate has Jesus flogged. Not content with this, the Roman soldiers seize the chance to express their hatred and contempt for the Jews by mocking his so-called kingship. Dressed up, battered and bleeding, taunted and alone, he is surely a sorry figure. Or is he? Just as when Caiaphas spoke more truly than he knew when he said it was best for one man to die for the people, so when Pilate says to the crowd, 'Behold the man!', he too speaks beyond his understanding.

'*Ecce homo*.' Caravaggio, Titian, Bosch, Daumier, Rubens and many other artists depict this episode in the life of Christ. 'Behold *the* man' – the man who, despite being the victim of injustice, at the mercy of his tormentors, heading for the most appalling death, is nevertheless the one who stands as the focal point of the world's history. He was there at its creation; he will be there at its ending; he is there as exemplar of all that we are created to be; he is the means of liberating us from all that would prevent us from realising our true destiny as children of God.

He is one with God, sharing his character and authority, yet he is also the body language of God, one with us, sharing our trials and temptations, our joys and sorrows, a man among men. *The* man.

But that is not how his accusers see Jesus. Ignoring Pilate's protests of innocence, they choose death. In every generation, we face the same choice: how to respond to this man?

Gracious God, many regard Jesus simply as a good man. Please reveal him to them as so much more than that: as the man, your Son, our Saviour, Lord and friend. Amen.

SHEILA WALKER

Misjudged

From then on Pilate tried to release him, but the Jews cried out, 'If you release this man, you are no friend of Caesar. Everyone who claims to be a king sets himself against Caesar'... They cried out , 'Away with him! Away with him! Crucify him!' Pilate asked them, 'Shall I crucify your King?' The chief priests answered, 'We have no king but Caesar.' Then he handed him over to them to be crucified.

Again we see the irony: the Roman governor seeking a just verdict for the Jewish preacher while the Jewish religious hierarchy sides with the Roman occupation. Furthermore, the priests have a trump card: if Pilate appears to be on the side of a rival of the emperor, his own life may be in jeopardy. It is possible that Pilate's position is already precarious, due to his connections with a discredited, rebellious imperial official, Sejanus. If so, this taunt will hit home even more forcefully, undermining his attempts to release Jesus.

The chief priests go further. Infuriated by Pilate's repeated reference to Jesus as king, they protest volubly that they have no king but Caesar. Like Pilate's '*Ecco homo*', their words echo down the ages with a significance unrecognised at the time. By declaring supreme allegiance to Caesar, they are not only protecting their own immediate interests, but denying the sovereign rule of God over them, his chosen people. Not only are they unable to acknowledge that Jesus, sharing the divine life, also shares the kingship of God over their lives, they also elevate the rule of Caesar over the authority of God, in any form.

While it is true that at times it may be right, or at least inevitable, to be pragmatic, it can be so tempting to allow the end to justify the means. Can this ever be right? A challenging debate, especially as here again we have the conundrum of God's redemption plan being precipitated by those who are rejecting him.

Life is complex: more grey than black and white. Lord, help us to make decisions which honour you, and trust you for the outcome, even when it may appear uncertain or disturbing. Amen.

SHEILA WALKER

Out of this world

Pilate also had an inscription written and put on the cross. It read, 'Jesus of Nazareth, the King of the Jews.' Many of the Jews read this inscription because the place where Jesus was crucified was near the city, and it was written in Hebrew, in Latin, and in Greek. Then the chief priests of the Jews said to Pilate, 'Do not write, "The King of the Jews," but, "This man said, I am King of the Jews."'

According to the Roman historian Josephus, crucifixion was the most wretched of deaths. For a start, the victim was made to carry his own crosspiece – not the whole cross (despite all those artistic representations to the contrary), since the upright posts would likely remain in place. Often the route was deliberately long, to prolong the agony and humiliation, and certainly Jesus needs help from Simon of Cyrene along the way.

A notice announcing the crime for which the condemned man is being crucified is placed in front of him: 'The King of the Jews.' Ambiguity again! Is Pilate being cynical? If this is really what the Jewish king looks like, a defenceless common criminal, then the Jews are indeed worthy of his contempt. Or does he have a sneaky feeling that there may just be some truth, or at least something unexplained, challenging even, about this so-called victim? He will refuse the plea from the chief priests to water down what he has written; for once, he will not waver or qualify his decision.

Interestingly, Jesus has been somewhat equivocal in his response to questions about his kingship, perhaps all too aware of the danger of misunderstandings. As we have seen, he makes the distinction that his kingdom is different from how the world would define or understand it. Pilate's words are true – but they call for a new interpretation, a new depth of understanding, a move beyond the temporal, the material, the political, to the eternal, the spiritual.

Jesus, lord of lords and king of kings, help us to discern the signs of your kingdom here among us and to live our lives in ways that will enable it to grow, knowing that one day every knee will bow to you. Amen.

SHEILA WALKER

Holistic

When the soldiers had crucified Jesus, they took his clothes and divided them into four parts, one for each soldier. They also took his tunic; now the tunic was seamless, woven in one piece from the top. So they said to one another, 'Let us not tear it but cast lots for it to see who will get it.' This was to fulfil what the scripture says, 'They divided my clothes among themselves, and for my clothing they cast lots.'

It was the usual practice for the four soldiers in the execution squad to share the victim's clothes after he has been stripped for crucifixion. Outer garment, sandals, head covering and belt will have been divided between them, leaving the seamless tunic. Seamless? This could indicate real quality – maybe an unusual find among those condemned to be crucified; perhaps they are prompted to ask themselves, 'Just who is this man?'

John is the only one of the gospel writers to record the echoes from Psalm 22:18, where David's words appear prophetic, one of many such references in the Old Testament, where Christ may be glimpsed as we read with the privilege of hindsight. It is a reminder that Jesus does not simply burst onto the scene at the moment of incarnation, but is an essential person of the Trinity since before the foundation of the world.

Thinking about Jesus' clothes, it is likely that his outer garments were very much like everyone else's, but perhaps it is not too fanciful to see a connection between that seamless undergarment and the seamlessness, the integrity, of his inner life – his thoughts, motivation, actions. He alone can lay claim to sinlessness, to perfect integration between outer and inner lives, an integration for which we all need to work and pray if we truly desire the transforming work of the Holy Spirit to make us more like him.

Gracious God, so often there is a painful disconnect between my inner and outer life; like Paul, I seem unable to do or to be all that I want to be – all that I know you want me to be. May I not feel condemned, but determined to be open to all that your Holy Spirit would work in me. Amen.

SHEILA WALKER

Heart-broken

Then the soldiers came and broke the legs of the first and of the other who had been crucified with him. But when they came to Jesus and saw that he was already dead, they did not break his legs. Instead, one of the soldiers pierced his side with a spear, and at once blood and water came out. (He who saw this has testified so that you also may believe. His testimony is true, and he knows that he tells the truth.)

As we saw yesterday, reading the Old Testament with the privilege of hindsight reveals many seemingly prophetic references to Jesus. Here, we have four more. First, the fact that, unusually, his legs are not broken, the usual practice to ensure the victim dies more quickly. In Exodus 12:46, the instruction for eating the Passover lamb is that not one of its bones shall be broken. And Jesus is the perfect Passover lamb, whose death is effective for all, forever. Psalm 34:20 also speaks of the Lord keeping all the bones of the righteous from being broken.

Zechariah 12:10 speaks of 'the one whom they [the inhabitants of Jerusalem] have pierced'. Mystifying, though, is the fact that when the soldier pierces Jesus' side, both blood and water emerge. Blood might be expected, if the spear pierces the heart, but water? Apparently, severe trauma can produce a clear fluid which collects around the heart; can it be, then, that Jesus dies as much from a broken heart as from the crucifixion itself, as he bears the sin and sorrow of the whole world?

John is anxious to underline the truth of this testimony – probably his own. It is important in this sceptical age to be assured that our faith rests on historical fact, attested by eyewitnesses. There is no doubt about the life and death of Jesus and, many would say, his resurrection. The question is, what do we make of them?

Lord Jesus, your heart was broken because of our sin; give us grace not to disappoint you now, as we seek to die to self and follow you, even to the cross and beyond. Amen.

SHEILA WALKER

Sacrifice

After these things, Joseph of Arimathea, who was a disciple of Jesus, though a secret one because of his fear of the Jews, asked Pilate to let him take away the body of Jesus. Pilate gave him permission, so he came and removed his body. Nicodemus, who had at first come to Jesus by night, also came, bringing a mixture of myrrh and aloes, weighing about a hundred pounds.

The bodies of those crucified would usually be consigned to a common criminals' burial plot outside the city, but Pilate is prepared to bend the rules. Again, there is ambiguity: is this the result of an uneasy conscience, antipathy towards the Jewish hierarchy, or the sovereignty of God? Or does it all amount to the same thing in the end?

What will it take to stir our faith into action? Both Joseph and Nicodemus are members of the Sanhedrin, but they are either absent when the council votes for Jesus' death or too fearful to speak out against the majority decision. It is never easy to be the odd one out, the one who will defend an unpopular opinion, the one who is, perhaps, prepared to be persecuted for Christ's sake. When we need the courage of our convictions and find it lacking, there is inevitably a question as to how firm those convictions are and how foundational in our lives.

Now we come to the cross and to the power of the cross. It is indeed a crossroads, insisting that we, along with Joseph and Nicodemus, must make a decision as to how we will respond to the death of this man who is either deluded, a charlatan or truly the Son of God. To their credit, they are both moved to step out in faith, putting their money where their mouth has previously failed to be and unwittingly helping to set the scene for a dramatic and challenging resurrection.

C.T. Studd, a missionary to China, famously said: 'If Christ be God and died for us, then no sacrifice can be too great for us to make for him.'

Lord Jesus, as we kneel before your cross, may we allow it to become the ground and inspiration for our living and dying. Amen.

SHEILA WALKER

Hebrews 8—13

 The writer of the epistle to the Hebrews draws on stories, objects and ways of worship associated with the first tabernacle. This tent travelled with the Hebrew people in the wilderness when they were led by Moses, after their escape from Egypt, and everything concerning it was carefully laid out in the law. The imagery would have been familiar to the readers of the epistle, who celebrated stories of their ancient ancestors at festivals, studied the law they were given and still followed similar patterns of worship.

As modern Christian readers, we can explore these references by looking back to where they appear in the Old Testament. However, for the writer of the epistle, these are only stepping stones into thinking about Christ's sacrifice on the cross, why it was significant and what kind of salvation it has brought about. Understanding what they are being compared with, and why, is more important than fully understanding the intricacies of the references themselves.

In a journey through the letter to the Hebrews, we keep passing the same landmarks: a tent, a mountain and a city. The writer compares the transient nature of the first tabernacle, in a tent in the wilderness, with the lasting and solid nature of the heavenly city. Later, the tent becomes a symbol of human life as the writer recalls the wandering heroes of faith, seeking their lasting city. Meanwhile, the mountain on which Moses met with God becomes a meeting place for God and Jesus, and finally the place where redeemed humanity can encounter God in a new and better way.

Throughout these chapters, there is constant comparison between the earthly and the heavenly things, and we are left with one word ringing in our ears: 'better'. In Christ we have been given a better covenant, with better promises, through better sacrifices; we are offered a better country and a better provision in a lasting city. The writer's excitement, gratitude and awe for what Jesus has achieved for us echo down the centuries in the words of this extraordinary letter.

AMY SCOTT ROBINSON

A sketch, a shadow and a pattern

Every high priest is appointed to offer gifts and sacrifices... They offer worship in a sanctuary that is a sketch and shadow of the heavenly one, just as Moses was warned when he was about to erect the tent. For, God said, 'See that you make everything according to the pattern that was shown you on the mountain.'

In the BBC television series *Fake or Fortune*, experts attempt to discern whether a work of art is truly by the well-known master its owners are hoping for or is a clever fake or copy. Very often, the piece in question is a sketch for an existing work of art. Going backwards in an artist's process and trying to discover whether these few pencil lines may have led to a famous oil painting is a fascinating and difficult business.

Here, the writer of Hebrews compares Moses' tabernacle of Exodus 26 with a sketch, a mere idea of the heavenly reality that exists, and with a shadow of that reality. While a sketch is made in preparation for something greater, a shadow is cast by the real thing. Shadows may give an idea of shape, but they are fuzzy, fleeting and colourless, and their size changes, too.

How can the tabernacle be both a preparation for the heavenly one and a fuzzy reflection of the real thing? The clue comes when the writer quotes Exodus 25:40, God telling Moses to follow the pattern that he was shown on the mountain, where he saw the glory of the Lord and received the law.

Along with the commandments, God's pattern for holy living, Moses received a pattern for worship based on the reality that already exists in heaven. A knitting pattern is just a selection of letters and numbers until it falls into the hands of a knitter, then it becomes a beautiful and functional garment. I wonder how it felt to Moses to worship in the tabernacle, while remembering the indescribable glory that he had seen on the mountain?

The writer of Hebrews says that the pattern of earthly worship, based on the true worship of heaven, finds its reality in Jesus.

Dear Lord, here we see through a glass darkly: our worship gives us fleeting experiences and shifting shadows of the true shape of you. Thank you that it all points us towards the solid, tangible reality of Jesus. Amen.

AMY SCOTT ROBINSON

A better covenant

This is the covenant that I will make with the house of Israel after those days, says the Lord: I will put my laws in their minds and write them on their hearts, and I will be their God, and they shall be my people. And they shall not teach one another or say to each other, 'Know the Lord,' for they shall all know me, from the least of them to the greatest.

I have been blessed with a musical family and many musical friends, and I love the visits when we bring out the instruments and play something together. Sometimes we follow sheet music and play duets by Baroque composers; other times we take the tune of a hymn or song that we all know by heart and play by ear, following the music wherever it takes us.

That is the difference between the old covenant and the one which the writer calls 'a better covenant' in Hebrews 8:6. Before, God's law had been external, written on stone tablets and followed dutifully, and when it was abandoned, all was lost. 'They did not continue in my covenant,' says God (v. 9). The strict demands of printed scores penned by musical maestros can cause a lesser musician like me to lose heart and give up altogether.

This new covenant, however, is internal, written on the hearts and minds of God's people, so that their knowledge of it is as complete and effortless as a familiar tune, a jazz standard that is the same and yet new every time.

Both methods of playing produce good music. There was nothing wrong with the old covenant in itself, but it could never fully meet the need of imperfect humanity. This new covenant, however, will lead to full knowledge of God and to complete forgiveness (vv. 11–12). And like a new piece of music striking up in a concert hall, it will cause the strains of the old one to fade away.

Father, I long to have your law written in my mind and on my heart; I long to know you better, to hear you clearly and to follow you closely in the twists and turns of my life. Thank you for that promise of your new, better covenant. Amen.

AMY SCOTT ROBINSON

Symbols of the present time

Behind the second curtain was a tent called the holy of holies. In it stood... the ark of the covenant overlaid on all sides with gold, in which there were a golden urn holding the manna, and Aaron's rod that budded, and the tablets of the covenant; above it were the cherubim of glory overshadowing the mercy seat... This is a symbol of the present time, indicating that gifts and sacrifices are offered that cannot perfect the conscience of the worshipper but deal only with food and drink and various baptisms, regulations for the body imposed until the time comes to set things right.

The ark of the covenant was not God, but it was God's chosen way of representing himself. It demonstrated his holiness and inspired awe. The power surrounding the ark won battles, toppled walls, opened rivers and struck down those who so much as touched it without the prescribed roles and rituals. Between the golden cherubim on top was the mercy seat, a place of meeting with God, the place of atonement. The description of it here glitters with repeated mentions of gold.

Inside this powerful symbol were more symbols, reminders of God's covenant with his people: their side of the covenant was written on the tablets of the law, while God's side appeared in the manna and Aaron's budding rod. These represented God's provision, intervention and guidance.

The writer of Hebrews gathers all these into one greater parable. The untouchable holiness of the ark, its place in the holy of holies, the need for blood offerings to approach it and the annual visit of the high priest were all a symbol, or parable, of the present time.

In other words, the instructions for worship themselves symbolised humanity's situation: separated by sin from God's shining perfection and holiness. The old covenant is a metaphor for humanity's need of a Messiah, which will be met in Jesus. All the instructions for worship and atonement point towards a problem that they themselves could not solve, and a reason to look for a time when God will set things right.

Father, when I get a glimpse of your sheer holiness, I am amazed by what you have done for me. Thank you for sending Jesus to set things right. Amen.

AMY SCOTT ROBINSON

Better sacrifice

Thus it was necessary for the sketches of the heavenly things to be purified with these rites, but the heavenly things themselves need better sacrifices than these. For Christ did not enter a sanctuary made by human hands, a mere copy of the true one, but he entered into heaven itself, now to appear in the presence of God on our behalf. Nor was it to offer himself again and again… But as it is, he has appeared once for all at the end of the ages to remove sin by the sacrifice of himself.

When my children were younger, we used to take a while to prepare them for new and unfamiliar situations. A first visit to the dentist, a holiday or a playgroup might all involve looking at photos of the new place, making a visual timetable of the day or playing through the possibilities with toys. All this helped them to know what to expect when faced with the situation itself.

That's how the writer of Hebrews sees the Aaronic rites and sacrifices, in contrast with 'the heavenly things themselves'. God's people have been shown to expect sacrifice for forgiveness and blood for atonement, but these were sketches. Now, for the reality of heaven, better sacrifices are needed.

We went through those preparations repeatedly until our children knew what to expect. But the real visit only had to happen once. Christ has not acted out a picture; he has done the thing itself. There is no need for a repeat.

To the writer of Hebrews, the sanctuary in the tabernacle was the equivalent of a toy doctor's surgery, where an experience can be played through and explained. But Jesus entered God's presence. In Greek, the word for 'presence' also means 'face', and is the same word Paul uses when he talks about seeing God face to face in 1 Corinthians 13:12.

Christ's sacrifice is not a rehearsal, but the real thing; not a photograph, but the real person. This better sacrifice does not purify only for a little while, but removes sin altogether, until Christ comes again to save all those who are eagerly awaiting him.

Lord, we thank you for your word and for all the stories of your love for your people. We praise you for your instructions about worship and holy living. Be with us whenever we read them, and show us how they can prepare us for a reality beyond our wildest dreams and hopes.

AMY SCOTT ROBINSON

A throne and a footstool

And every priest stands day after day at his service, offering again and again the same sacrifices that can never take away sins. But when Christ had offered for all time a single sacrifice for sins, 'he sat down at the right hand of God,' and since then has been waiting 'until his enemies would be made a footstool for his feet.' For by a single offering he has perfected for all time those who are sanctified.

After running a book stall at an indoor market for three days, my knees, feet and back were complaining loudly. For some people, standing up all day is an ordinary requirement of work, but for this sedentary writer, it had come as a shock! My voice, too, was failing, after repeating the same sales patter to every passing customer, all delivered with the same big smile until my cheeks were sore. Sinking into an armchair for the first time every evening was a wonderful relief.

Remembering that experience, I feel very sorry for the priests in this passage who stand up day after day, offering repeated but ineffective sacrifices. The job of a priest was gruelling, gory and complicated – just read Leviticus 16 and imagine how long the strenuous process must have taken. Christ, on the other hand, offers his sacrifice and then sits down – and puts his feet up! It is a deliberate contrast, the throne and footstool instead of the constant standing and work.

Yet Christ sits enthroned at the right hand of God on behalf of those who have been standing. Those who are sanctified through this new covenant are perfected for all time (Hebrews 10:14). Christ's sacrifice puts an end to the need for all the repetition and slog, the intense work that will never be perfect no matter how hard we try. Ephesians 2:6 says that we will be 'seated in heavenly places' with him. Because of Jesus, we can all sit down and rest.

Dear Jesus, you said that your yoke is easy and your burden is light, and that those who come to you can find rest for their souls. Help me understand what you meant – and what you went through to make those words true. Thank you that we can sit together. Amen.

AMY SCOTT ROBINSON

Hopeful and faithful

Since we have confidence to enter the sanctuary by the blood of Jesus… and since we have a great priest over the house of God, let us approach with a true heart in full assurance of faith… Let us hold fast to the confession of our hope without wavering, for he who has promised is faithful. And let us consider how to provoke one another to love and good deeds.

The planning started months before his birthday. From the moment his parents promised to buy him the new world-building computer game, the soon-to-be 10-year-old had started to fill notebooks with details of his campaigns, sketches of buildings and designs for maps, so that by the time the great day came, he would be ready with months' worth of plans and ideas for his new programme. He could not wait to get stuck in.

Hebrews 10:23–24 contains both faith and hope, but it is interesting to see which word belongs to whom. We are told to hold fast to hope without wavering, because the one who has promised is faithful. Holding on tight to something can only be helpful if the thing itself is rock solid and will support us. The writer implies that God always keeps his promises, and because we know that he has kept and will keep them in Jesus, we can have confidence (v. 19) and assurance (v. 22). Like a little boy who unquestioningly trusts his parents when they promise to give him the game he asked for, we can be hopeful because we know God is faithful.

And, like that little boy, holding fast to hope is not just an empty experience of waiting, but something which shows in our actions. In the next verses, the writer of Hebrews urges us to 'provoke one another into love and good deeds', to meet together and encourage one another, because we are all looking forward to the same day together. Talking about it, planning for it and rejoicing in it can all take place before the day arrives. It's a day on which Christ will come to save those who are waiting for him with hope. A day on which God will set everything right. A day promised by one who is faithful.

Dear Father, thank you that you are faithful and keep all your promises. Thank you that we have eternal hope in Jesus. Help us to encourage one another in that hope, letting it show in our thoughts, actions and conversation until the great day arrives. Amen.

AMY SCOTT ROBINSON

A better country

They confessed that they were strangers and foreigners on the earth, for people who speak in this way make it clear that they are seeking a homeland. If they had been thinking of the land that they had left behind, they would have had opportunity to return. But as it is, they desire a better homeland, that is, a heavenly one. Therefore God is not ashamed to be called their God; indeed, he has prepared a city for them.

We stood back and surveyed the empty hallway. Our possessions had all been driven to our new house, we had scrubbed the children's scribbles off the walls, and now there was nothing to do but lock the door behind us a final time. After moving from student life to curacy, a first post in ministry, never staying in the same place longer than three years, this house where we had spent a decade had really felt like home – but an exciting and beautiful new one was waiting for us.

Here, the writer of Hebrews imagines the patriarchs – Abraham and Sarah, Isaac and Jacob – dwelling in tents and moving constantly through foreign lands. Instead of thinking of what they had left behind, they kept moving onwards, showing that they were people seeking a promised land where they could settle. Like so many other aspects of these Old Testament stories, the writer interprets this spiritually: the better country that was waiting for these wanderers, and is waiting for all Christians, is a heavenly city.

The contrast between the temporary flimsiness of a tent and the permanent solidity of a city is the same contrast as the one in the earlier chapters, between Moses' first tabernacle and a heavenly sanctuary and throne room. For the writer of Hebrews, the Christian life is always moving away from the sketch and towards the reality, leaving behind temporary things to enter eternity. Far from being insubstantial and spiritual, for this writer, heaven is far more solid and lasting than earth can ever be.

Father, sometimes life can feel fleeting and fragile. We miss the things and the people we have left behind. Thank you that you have prepared a place for us in a heavenly city, where all good things will last and our travels will finally end. Amen.

AMY SCOTT ROBINSON

A montage of heroes

Time would fail me to tell of Gideon, Barak, Samson, Jephthah, of David and Samuel and the prophets, who through faith conquered kingdoms, administered justice, obtained promises, shut the mouths of lions, quenched the power of fire, escaped the edge of the sword, were made strong out of weakness, became mighty in war, put foreign armies to flight… Yet all these… did not receive what was promised, since God had provided something better so that they would not, apart from us, be made perfect.

Hebrews 11:32–40 is quite a list of miracles and feats of endurance. The writer, having already talked about the patriarchs and Moses, now enthusiastically describes heroes of the faith from Gideon onwards. With a few words, familiar stories spring to life: Daniel in the lion's den; epic battles fought and won; Elijah and Elisha raising the widows' sons from death. Then follows a list of the persecution suffered by these faithful few: imprisonments, graphic martyrdoms and banishment.

Yet at the end of this montage of remarkable, faithful people, the writer states that even these heroes did not receive what was promised. Although they lived in hope, knowing God's promises, they did not live to see Jesus as Messiah and the unfolding of God's salvation plan. It reminds me of Simeon in Luke 2:28–32, recognising just how blessed he was to have lived long enough to hold the infant Jesus in his arms. However, for the writer of Hebrews, God's plan was better both for these heroes of the faith and for us, because although the old covenant could not make any human perfect, the salvation of Jesus will make the whole of creation perfect together.

It would be easy to read this passage and feel inadequate. These heroes achieved and suffered so much without even knowing how God's promise of rescue would be fulfilled. Yet when the camera pans out from the montage of each individual life to the big picture of God's plan, we can see that our lives also fit into a much bigger and better story – and, wonderfully, we do know how that promise was achieved.

Dear God, thank you for making me a part of your plan for all creation. Thank you for showing me Jesus. Amen.

AMY SCOTT ROBINSON

Run with perseverance

Therefore, since we are surrounded by so great a cloud of witnesses, let us also lay aside every weight and the sin that clings so closely, and let us run with perseverance the race that is set before us, looking to Jesus, the pioneer and perfecter of our faith, who for the sake of the joy that was set before him endured the cross, disregarding its shame, and has taken his seat at the right hand of the throne of God.

As a child, teacher and parent I have witnessed many school sports days, but the most moving one was a few years ago. A child with obvious physical disabilities lined up to race with her class. Children can be unkind, but not here: this child was obviously the hero of the hour. Before the race even began, the rest of the school was chanting her name from the stands. As each competitor crossed the finish line, they ran to the side of the track and cheered their classmate on as she hobbled forwards with her walking frame. By the time she finished, about five minutes after the rest, she was surrounded by enthusiastic friends congratulating her for her achievement.

That's the picture which sums up 39 verses about heroes of faith. However far behind we are and however slowly we are going, this cloud of witnesses has run the race before us, and now they are praising our perseverance as we press on. Running with perseverance is not about being the best runner. It is about pushing forwards against our limits – those weights, that sin that clings – and reaching the finish.

While the cheers from the side encourage us, the writer suggests that the best way to reach that line is to keep our eyes on Jesus. He has run the race too, making a way for us; and while his example gives us strength, it is his seat on the throne of God that lets us know that we can and will finish the race and be welcomed to sit with him.

Dear Jesus, keep my eyes fixed on you as I run. Thank you that I know you will be waiting for me at the finish line.

AMY SCOTT ROBINSON

Two mountains

You have not come to something that can be touched, a blazing fire, and darkness, and gloom, and a tempest... But you have come to Mount Zion and to the city of the living God, the heavenly Jerusalem, and to innumerable angels in festal gathering... and to Jesus, the mediator of a new covenant, and to the sprinkled blood that speaks a better word than the blood of Abel.

At the very end of Charles Dickens' *A Christmas Carol*, there is a scene when Bob Cratchit arrives late to work. His boss, the previously mean and miserly Ebenezer Scrooge, decides to have a bit of fun with Bob, who has no idea that Scrooge is now reformed. Scowling, Scrooge tells his terrified employee: 'I am not going to stand this sort of thing any longer. And therefore... I am about to raise your salary!'

Because of Jesus, our expectations of our reception with God have entirely changed. For Moses, God's presence on the mountain was darkness and storm and a voice so terrifying that it could not be endured. Now, entering the presence of God is like arriving in a heavenly city, full of angels having a party. It is like expecting to be fired and getting a promotion instead, or like a child called to the head teacher's office, expecting to be in trouble, and instead receiving an award. We deserve punishment but are given mercy.

The writer of Hebrews contrasts the blood of Abel and the blood of Jesus. When Abel was murdered by his brother Cain, God told Cain that his brother's blood cried out to him from the ground (Genesis 4:10). From then on, we should expect bloodshed to become a voice of accusation, calling out to God for justice. But the blood of Jesus 'speaks a better word', because it cries out to God on our behalf for forgiveness.

The new mountain cancels out the old one; Jesus' blood drowns out the voice of Abel's blood, and we are welcomed into an undeserved and unexpected reward.

Dear God, thank you for your mercy and your love. Instead of fear, we can look forward to festivity; instead of a terrifying voice, we will hear your gentle words of welcome. Thank you! Amen.

AMY SCOTT ROBINSON

A lasting city

Therefore Jesus also suffered outside the city gate in order to sanctify the people by his own blood. Let us then go to him outside the camp and bear the abuse he endured. For here we have no lasting city, but we are looking for the city that is to come. Through him, then, let us continually offer a sacrifice of praise to God, that is, the fruit of lips that confess his name.

In February 2020, two cheetahs named Saba and Nairo were flown 6,000 miles from Howletts Wild Animal Park in Kent to South Africa to begin a process of rewilding. Once there, they were housed first in a cheetah sanctuary, while they got used to the new climate, then in a private reserve, where they were monitored while learning to hunt for themselves. Gradually they became ready to be released into the true wild.

Outside the city walls of the ancient world, everything that was undesirable or potentially polluting was gathered. Animals that had been sacrificed for sin were burnt, the dead were buried, criminals were executed and rubbish was thrown away. A little further out were small communities of people with contagious diseases. When verse 13 tells us to go and find Jesus outside the camp, it is asking us to leave behind everything familiar, clean and comfortable and step into a world of unpredictability and danger – and we follow in Jesus' footsteps when we obey.

But the following verse returns to an idea the writer of Hebrews has been repeating throughout the last few chapters. We only leave this city to seek a better one. This world may feel solid, but it is flimsy and fleeting compared with heaven. In leaving the illusion of safety and comfort, we find something even better and more lasting.

The cheetahs stepped away from the enclosure where they had been fed and monitored, and walked for the first time into the wild, where they truly belonged. Like them, when we risk a step towards Jesus, we take a step into true freedom and eternal safety – wherever he calls us.

Jesus, you call me from outside the city. You call me out of familiar patterns and comfortable assumptions to discover that your kingdom is more real, more lasting and much more exciting than anything this world has to offer. Lead me outside the city walls and deeper into your eternal truth. Amen.

AMY SCOTT ROBINSON

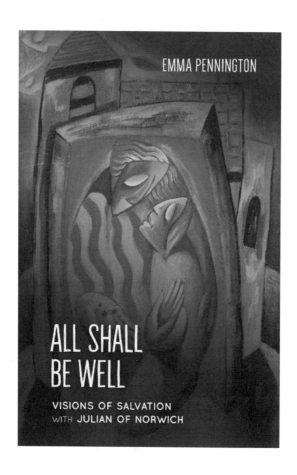

How can all be well in the world in which we live? What does 'All shall be well' mean when all is not well? Through revelations ten to sixteen of her *Revelations of Divine Love*, Julian of Norwich returns time and again to the idea that 'all is well'. In her latest book Emma Pennington examines this popular mantra and explores what Julian really means by it, bringing depth and relevance to these words for the reader who lives in an age of pandemic, war and climate crisis which closely echoes Julian's own. Through deep engagement with Julian's visions of salvation Emma encourages the reader to reflect in prayer and devotion on their own personal relationship with God.

All Shall Be Well
Visions of salvation with Julian of Norwich
Emma Pennington
978 1 80039 206 9 £12.99
brfonline.org.uk

SHARING OUR VISION – MAKING A GIFT

I would like to make a donation to support BRF Ministries.
Please use my gift for:

☐ Where the need is greatest   ☐ Anna Chaplaincy   ☐ Living Faith
☐ Messy Church   ☐ Parenting for Faith

Title	First name/initials	Surname

Address

Postcode

Email

Telephone

Signature

Date

Please accept my gift of:

☐ £2   ☐ £5   ☐ £10   ☐ £20   Other £ ☐

by (*delete as appropriate*):

☐ Cheque/Charity Voucher payable to 'BRF'
☐ MasterCard/Visa/Debit card/Charity card

Name on card

Card no. ☐☐☐☐ ☐☐☐☐ ☐☐☐☐ ☐☐☐☐

Expires end M M Y Y   Security code* ☐☐☐   *Last 3 digits on the reverse of the card

Signature

Date

Please complete other side of form ➲

BRF Ministries Gift Aid Declaration

In order to Gift Aid your donation, you must tick the box below.

☐ I want to Gift Aid my donation and any donation I make in the future or have made in the past four years to BRF Ministries

I am a UK taxpayer and understand that if I pay less Income Tax and/or Capital Gains Tax in the current tax year than the amount of Gift Aid claimed on all my donations, it is my responsibility to pay any difference.

Please notify BRF Ministries if you want to cancel this Gift Aid declaration, change your name or home address, or no longer pay sufficient tax on your income and/or capital gains.

You can also give online at **brf.org.uk/donate**, which reduces our administration costs, making your donation go further.

Our ministry is only possible because of the generous support of individuals, churches, trusts and gifts in wills.

☐ I would like to leave a gift to BRF Ministries in my will. Please send me further information.

☐ I would like to find out about giving a regular gift to BRF Ministries.

For help or advice regarding making a gift, please contact our fundraising team +44 (0)1235 462305

Your privacy

We will use your personal data to process this transaction. From time to time we may send you information about the work of BRF Ministries that we think may be of interest to you. Our privacy policy is available at **brf.org.uk/privacy**. Please contact us if you wish to discuss your mailing preferences.

Registered with

FUNDRAISING **REGULATOR**

 Please complete other side of form

Please return this form to 'Freepost BRF'
No other address information or stamp is needed

Bible Reading Fellowship is a charity (233280) and company limited by guarantee (301324), registered in England and Wales

Reading *New Daylight* in a group

GORDON GILES

It is good to talk. The Rule of Benedict, which formed the spiritual foundations of the daily prayer life of so many ecclesiastical foundations, recommended daily scripture reading as a key aspect of the community life of work and prayer, and during Lent especially each monk was allocated a book to read daily. While Benedict's monks did not talk much, nowadays discussion and reflection can be helpful and enlightening when reading passages that others are reading simultaneously. Separated by space, as each reads alone, we are yet connected by the common food of scripture, taken in our own time at our own pace. We each chew on it in our own way, and we can all learn from each other's insights and interpretations.

To assist with that, here are some 'open' questions that may enable discussion in a Bible study or other group who gather to take further what is published here. The same questions may also aid personal devotion. Use them as you wish, and may God bless and inspire you on your journey as you read, mark and inwardly digest holy words to ponder and nourish the soul.

General discussion starters

These can be used for any study series within this issue. Remember there are no right or wrong answers – these questions are simply to enable a group to engage in conversation.

- What do you think is the main idea or theme of the author in this series? Did that come across strongly?

- Have any of the issues discussed touched on personal – or shared – aspects of your life?

- What evidence or stories do the authors draw on to illuminate, or be illuminated by the passages of scripture.

- Which do you prefer: scripture informing daily modern life, or modern life shining a new light on scripture?

- Does the author 'call you to action' in a realistic and achievable way? Do you think their ideas will work in the secular world?

- Have any specific passages struck you? If so, how and why, do you think? Is God speaking to you through scripture and reflection?
- Was anything completely new to you? Any 'eureka' or jaw-dropping moments? If so, what difference will that make?

Questions for group discussion

Luke 10—12 (Tim Heaton)

- Try to retell the parable of the good Samaritan in our own time and place. Who might the priest, Levite and Samaritan be today?
- Are you by nature a Martha or a Mary?
- How does evil manifest itself in the world today? (Try to think beyond demons and the occult.)
- In what ways are you a light in the world? Share with the group some of the things you do that bring light to others.
- What do you worry about that perhaps you shouldn't be worrying about? What might be done to ease your anxiety?
- Have you ever experienced conflict with family, friends or neighbours because of your faith? Talk about it if you feel able to.

Joel (Ross Moughtin)

- Joel had an extensive knowledge of scripture, which he used in understanding his nation's crisis. How has your knowledge of scripture helped you understand a pressing problem or challenge?
- Why do we find it so difficult to confront reality? What strategies do we use? How may our faith in God and our fellow Christians help?
- Share any experience you may have had when your very foundations were shaken. How did you encounter God in this situation? What did you learn?
- 'Rend your hearts and not your clothing' (Joel 2:13, NRSV). Why do we find it so hard to repent? What does true repentance mean?
- Joel addresses his message to animals and even to the soil. What does this teach us about our relationship to the environment?
- What is your response to Joel's prophecy of the Holy Spirit being breathed into every living being?

Wilderness psalms: Psalms 30—40 (Tony Horsfall)

- Which of the psalms in this section did you enjoy most? How did it help you?
- Which of the psalms here did you find difficult? Why was that?
- Gather together the references to Jesus in these psalms. What do you learn about him?
- What do we learn about prayer as we read these psalms?
- David had an open and frank relationship with God. Can you give examples? What do you feel about this as a pattern for your walk with God?
- What have you learned about God's character and ways?
- Do you agree that busyness can be a form of escapism, preventing us from thinking about the brevity of life? Do you see this tendency in your own life?
- The psalmist says, 'Do not fret' (Psalm 37:1). What makes you anxious? How can your faith bring calmness to you?
- What testimony do you have to share about the goodness of God? How might you communicate it to others?
- David was a great songwriter and singing has always played a large part in Christian worship. What hymn or song has helped, inspired or challenged you?

Hebrews 8—13 (Amy Scott Robinson)

- 'Now the main point in what we are saying is this: we have such a high priest, one who is seated at the right hand of the throne of the Majesty in the heavens' (Hebrews 8:1, NRSV). Does this image change the way you usually picture Jesus? How, and why do you think that is?
- 'But Jesus has now obtained a more excellent ministry, and to that degree he is the mediator of a better covenant, which has been enacted on the basis of better promises' (Hebrews 8:6). The word 'better' occurs multiple times in the book of Hebrews. Can you list some of the ways that Jesus makes things better – either for the whole world or for you personally?

- 'Now faith is the assurance of things hoped for, the conviction of things not seen' (Hebrews 11:1). What are some of your biggest hopes? Would you change anything in your day-to-day life if you could know for sure that those hopes would come true?

- Hebrews 11 is a list of many heroes of the faith. Who are some of your heroes? What are their stories, and what makes you admire them?

- 'If they had been thinking of the land that they had left behind, they would have had opportunity to return. But as it is, they desire a better homeland, that is, a heavenly one' (Hebrews 11:15–16). What have you left behind in your spiritual journey? What have you set your heart on?

- 'Therefore, since we are receiving a kingdom that cannot be shaken, let us show gratitude' (Hebrews 12:28). What things from these readings have made you feel grateful to God?

Meet the authors

The notes on artificial intelligence are written by different people, coming together to reflect on a common theme. They have done so under the banner of The Faraday Institute for Science and Religion, a Cambridge-based interdisciplinary research institute improving public understanding of science and religion.

The Faraday Institute derives its name from Michael Faraday (1791–1867), one of Britain's best-known scientists, who saw his faith as integral to his scientific research. Its main focus is on the relationship between science and the Christian faith, but it also engages with those of any faith or none. Founded as part of St Edmund's College in 2006, since 2018 it has been an independent charitable organisation and an associate member of the Cambridge Theological Federation.

The mission of The Faraday Institute is to shed new light on life's big questions through academically rigorous research in the field of science and religion; to provide life-changing resources for those with interests in science and faith through research dissemination, education and training; and to catalyse a change in attitude towards science and faith, through outreach to schools, colleges, the scientific community, religious institutions and the general public. It has a vision to make the very best of academic scholarship available as widely as possible.

Find out more about The Faraday Institute for Science and Religion at **faraday.cam.ac.uk/about/overview**

For the set of reflections on artificial intelligence a team of contributors were invited to write:

- **Ruth Bancewicz, Mike Brownnutt** and **Graham Budd** are based at The Faraday Institute.
- **Chris Goswami** is a Baptist pastor and former tech sector executive.
- **Rachel Siow Robertson** is a philosopher at Hong Kong Baptist University.
- **Tim Bull** is a canon at St Albans Cathedral and a software engineer.
- **Nathan Mladin** is a theologian at Theos.
- **Patricia Shaw** is a lawyer and AI ethicist.

- **Gordon Giles**, editor of *New Daylight*, is canon chancellor at Rochester Cathedral and a musician and philosopher.
- **Ian Morrison** is a neurologist and Church of Scotland minister.
- **John Wyatt** is a neonatologist and ethicist.
- **Charmaine Mhlanga** is a Baptist pastor and former care home manager.
- **Justin Tomkins** is a Church of England priest and scientist.
- **Murdo Macdonald** is a scientist who runs the Church of Scotland Society Religion and Technology project.
- **Peter Robinson** is emeritus professor of computer technology and president of Gonville and Caius College, University of Cambridge.

Recommended reading

There is no doubt that each of us has a place in the Easter story, but what happened on the cross is not just a story of me and Jesus. It is far deeper and wider than that.

In *The Whole Easter Story*, BRF Ministries' 2025 Lent book, Jo Swinney explores the broader impact of the Easter story on God's relationship with creation. Through Bible readings, reflections and stories from A Rocha's global conservation efforts (including illustrations of species they work to support), discover how the cross transforms not just our own individual connection with Jesus, but also our relationships with each other and our world.

The following is an edited extract taken from the reading for Day 1. Entitled 'Created', it is a reflection on Psalm 139:13–16.

I have twice had the strange experience of growing a human in my body. At first the only evidence of their existence was a pink line on a plastic stick. After a few weeks they made me feel very sick, and then they grew big enough to give me a bump and a great deal of discomfort. When I look at my teenage daughters, I find it hard to connect these beautiful, fully grown, and increasingly independent people with anything that might have gone on inside me. We may have sophisticated scanning equipment now that makes the womb slightly less secret, but I can still relate to the idea that babies develop in 'the depths of the earth', a process shrouded in mystery and deep darkness.

I can also confirm that I was not a consciously active participant in the task of taking Alexa and Charis from being a couple of cells to fully formed babies. It was God who created them, who breathed life into their beings, who gave them their fingerprints, their temperaments, their quirks and tendencies. As humans we have become very clever in certain regards. We know our bodies are composed of eleven elements (oxygen, hydrogen, nitrogen, carbon, calcium, phosphorus, sulphur, potassium, sodium, chlorine, and magnesium, in case you were wondering). But we have no clue how to combine those elements into a living, breathing, emotional and spiritual being.

As we begin to consider our relationship with God in the context of the Easter story, a good place to start is with the fact he is creator, and we are created. We were created as homo sapiens, a distinct species among many, imprinted with the very image of God (Genesis 1:27), and we were each and every one of us created, seen, significant and loved before one of our days came to be.

I have heard the story told from a different starting point, as I imagine you have. Sometimes it is told like this: people are awful; we are dirty, sinful, horrid things, and we took God right to the end of his tether, so he had to come and die for us.

I found a website giving step-by-step instructions for evangelism, and this is step two (step one was about sin too):

> Write the word 'SIN' vertically between the words 'MAN' and 'GOD'. Quote Romans 3:23 – 'For all have sinned and fall short of the glory of God.' Questions to ask: 'What does the word "all" in this verse mean? Does it include you?' Always use questions after giving a verse so that you may know whether its truth is getting across. Say, 'Since God is holy and man is sinful, sin separates man from God.'

But the Bible doesn't start with sin; it starts with creation, and that makes all the difference to how we understand our relationship with God. Let's dig into Psalm 139 and you'll see what I mean.

Psalms are songs reflecting the experience of their authors' lives with God and infused with references to early sections of scripture, books of history, prophecy, poetry and apocalypse. They were written long before the life of Jesus, but in the understanding that all too often humankind was failing, corporately and individually, to keep their side of the covenant promises that framed their relationship with God. King David led his people into so many bloody battles that he was forbidden from building a temple. His relationship history would definitely have earned him a well-deserved 'Love Rat' tabloid splash. He worshipped God with all his heart but sometimes cursed him too. In all this complexity, one thing was clear: as a being created by God, he knew his intrinsic worth was never up for debate – 'Your works are wonderful' (v. 14).

David's language in Psalm 139 describes a very hands-on process of making – he uses words like 'knitted' and 'woven'. These crafts involve patterns, but patterns which allow for creativity. Each human is like others, and at the same time unique. We are wired with a need for significance, to have a place, to be seen and known as an individual, not just a speck in a blurry crowd of billions, and thankfully we have a God with the capacity to relate to each of us – 'Your eyes saw [me]… all the days ordained for me were written in your book' (v. 16). We can base our self-esteem on everything from an annual appraisal at work, to the number of hearts under our Instagram posts, to how many people show up to our birthday drinks, but why would we? Each of us has been 'fearfully and wonderfully made' (v. 14) by our ever-loving creator God.

For reflection

Think about some of the people who have shaped how you see yourself, from parents to teachers, to friends and spouses, to employers and media figures. How much power have you given their voices? How can you let God's voice speak more loudly, and what would change if you decided to listen only to him when it comes to your worth?

Prayer

Abba, Father, I am yours. You meant me to be here, and you look at me with love and pleasure. Your knowledge of me is deeper than I can fathom. My feelings, motivations and impulses are laid bare before you. I can't deceive you; I can't hide from you. Thank you that your commitment to me is unshakeable. Amen.

Salish sucker *(Catostomus sp. cf. catostomus)*

A small freshwater fish thought to be locally extinct – until it was identified in the Little Campbell River watershed (British Columbia, Canada) in 2011! The population is now thriving.

To order a copy of The Whole Easter Story, use the order form opposite or visit **brfonline.org.uk**

To order

Online: **brfonline.org.uk**
Telephone: +44 (0)1865 319700
Mon–Fri 9.30–17.00

Delivery times within the UK are normally 15 working days. Prices are correct at the time of going to press but may change without prior notice.

Title	Price	Qty	Total
Sharing the Easter Story	£8.99		
Journey to Contentment	£8.99		
Holding Onto Hope	£12.99		
Knowing You, Jesus – 365 Devotional	£19.99		
All Shall Be Well	£12.99		
The Whole Easter Story – BRF Ministries Lent book	£9.99		

POSTAGE AND PACKING CHARGES			
Order value	UK	Europe	Rest of world
Under £7.00	£2.00	Available on request	Available on request
£7.00–£29.99	£3.00		
£30.00 and over	FREE		

Total value of books	
Postage and packing	
Donation*	
Total for this order	

* Please complete and return the Gift Aid declaration on page 142.

Please complete in BLOCK CAPITALS

Title _____ First name/initials _____ Surname _____

Address _____

_____ Postcode _____

Acc. No. _____ Telephone _____

Email _____

Method of payment

☐ Cheque (made payable to BRF) ☐ MasterCard / Visa

Card no. ☐☐☐☐ ☐☐☐☐ ☐☐☐☐ ☐☐☐☐

Expires end ☐☐ ☐☐ Security code ☐☐☐ Last 3 digits on the reverse of the card

We will use your personal data to process this order. From time to time we may send you information about the work of BRF Ministries. Please contact us if you wish to discuss your mailing preferences. Our privacy policy is available at **brf.org.uk/privacy**.

Please return this form to:

BRF Ministries, 15 The Chambers, Vineyard, Abingdon OX14 3FE | **enquiries@brf.org.uk**
For terms and cancellation information, please visit **brfonline.org.uk/terms**.

Bible Reading Fellowship (BRF) is a charity (233280) and company limited by guarantee (301324), registered in England and Wales

BRF Ministries needs you!

If you're one of our many thousands of regular *New Daylight* readers you will know all about the impact that regular Bible reading has your faith and the value of daily notes to guide, inform and inspire you. Here are some recent comments from *New Daylight* readers:

> 'Thank you for all the many inspiring writings that help so much when things are tough.'

> 'Just right for me – I learned a lot!'

> 'We looked forward to each day's message as we pondered each passage and comment.'

If you have similarly positive things to say about *New Daylight*, would you be willing to share your experience with others? Perhaps you could give a short talk or write a brief article about why you find *New Daylight* so helpful. You could form a *New Daylight* reading group, perhaps supplying members with their first copy of the notes. Or you could pass on your back copies or give someone a gift subscription. However you do it, the important thing is to find creative ways to put a copy of *New Daylight* into someone else's hands.

It doesn't need to be complicated and we can help with group and bulk-buy discounts.

We can supply further information if you need it and and would love to hear about it if you do find ways to get *New Daylight* into new readers' hands.

For more information:

- Email **enquiries@brf.org.uk**
- Phone us on **+44 (0)1865 319700** Mon–Fri 9.30–17.00
- Write to us at BRF Ministries, 15 The Chambers, Vineyard, Abingdon OX14 3FE

Inspiring people of all ages to grow in Christian faith

At BRF Ministries, we long for people of all ages to grow in faith and understanding of the Bible. That's what all our work as a charity is about.

- Our **Living Faith** range of resources helps Christians go deeper in their understanding of scripture, in prayer and in their walk with God. Our conferences and events bring people together to share this journey, while our Holy Habits resources help whole congregations grow together as disciples of Jesus, living out and sharing their faith.

- We also want to make it easier for local churches to engage effectively in ministry and mission – by helping them bring new families into a growing relationship with God through **Messy Church** or by supporting churches as they nurture the spiritual life of older people through **Anna Chaplaincy**.

- Our **Parenting for Faith** team coaches parents and others to raise God-connected children and teens, and enables churches to fully support them.

Do you share our vision?

Though a significant proportion of BRF Ministries' funding is generated through our charitable activities, we are dependent on the generous support of individuals, churches and charitable trusts.

If you share our vision, would you help us to enable even more people of all ages to grow in faith? Your prayers and financial support are vital for the work that we do. You could:

- support us with a regular donation or one-off gift
- consider leaving a gift to BRF Ministries in your will
- encourage your church to support us as part of your church's giving to home mission – perhaps focusing on a specific ministry or programme
- most important of all, support us with your prayers.

Donate at **brf.org.uk/donate** or use the form on pages 141–42.

God is in control

Then Job answered the Lord: 'I know that you can do all things and that no purpose of yours can be thwarted.'
JOB 42:1–2 (NRSV)

We sometimes forget the more cheerful ending of the book of Job. As we have continued to live through challenging times, be that on personal, national and international levels, the reminder that God has it all under control is a reassuring promise to hold on to.

In this season, the Living Faith team are providing materials for Lent and Easter, and our collection of Easter and everyday cards is growing. Meanwhile, resources for Advent and Christmas are also being prepared.

The Anna Chaplaincy, Messy Church and Parenting for Faith teams continue to offer training, resources and events supporting individuals and churches with their invaluable work, which really does enable people to grow in Christian faith across all ages and to know God cannot be thwarted.

We believe this work is invaluable, and we are assured of this by the kind feedback we receive. However, none of this would be possible without kind donations from individuals, churches, charitable trusts and gifts in wills. If you would like to support us now and in the future you can become a Friend of BRF Ministries by making a monthly gift of £2 a month or more – we thank you for your friendship.

Find out more at **brf.org.uk/donate** or get in touch with us on **01235 462305** or via **giving@brf.org.uk**.

We thank you for your support and your prayers.

The fundraising team at BRF Ministries

Give. Pray. Get involved.
brf.org.uk

NEW DAYLIGHT SUBSCRIPTION RATES

Please note our new subscription rates, current until 30 April 2026:

Individual subscriptions
covering 3 issues for under 5 copies, payable in advance
(including postage & packing):

	UK	Europe	Rest of world
New Daylight	£21.30	£29.55	£35.25
New Daylight 3-year subscription (9 issues) (not available for Deluxe)	£60.30	N/A	N/A
New Daylight Deluxe per set of 3 issues p.a.	£26.55	£36.00	£44.10

Group subscriptions
covering 3 issues for 5 copies or more, sent to one UK address (post free):

New Daylight	£15.75 per set of 3 issues p.a.
New Daylight Deluxe	£19.50 per set of 3 issues p.a.

Please note that the annual billing period for group subscriptions runs from 1 May to 30 April.

Overseas group subscription rates
Available on request. Please email **enquiries@brf.org.uk**.

Copies may also be obtained from Christian bookshops:

New Daylight	£5.25 per copy
New Daylight Deluxe	£6.50 per copy

> All our Bible reading notes can be ordered online by visiting **brfonline.org.uk/subscriptions**

NEW DAYLIGHT INDIVIDUAL SUBSCRIPTION FORM

> To set up a recurring subscription, please go to
> **brfonline.org.uk/nd-subscription**

Title _____ First name/initials _____ Surname _____

Address _____

_____ Postcode _____

Telephone _____ Email _____

Please send *New Daylight* beginning with the May 2025 / September 2025 / January 2026 issue (*delete as appropriate*):

(*please tick box*)	UK	Europe	Rest of world
New Daylight 1-year subscription	☐ £21.30	☐ £29.55	☐ £35.25
New Daylight 3-year subscription	☐ £60.30	N/A	N/A
New Daylight Deluxe	☐ £26.55	☐ £36.00	☐ £44.10

Optional donation to support the work of BRF Ministries £ _____

Total enclosed £ _____ (cheques should be made payable to 'BRF')

Please complete and return the Gift Aid declaration on page 142 to make your donation even more valuable to us.

Please charge my MasterCard / Visa with £ _____

Card no. ☐☐☐☐ ☐☐☐☐ ☐☐☐☐ ☐☐☐☐

Expires end ☐☐☐☐ (MM YY)   Security code ☐☐   Last 3 digits on the reverse of the card

We will use your personal data to process this order. From time to time we may send you information about the work of BRF Ministries. Please contact us if you wish to discuss your mailing preferences. Our privacy policy is available at **brf.org.uk/privacy**.

Please return this form with the appropriate payment to:
BRF Ministries, 15 The Chambers, Vineyard, Abingdon OX14 3FE
For terms and cancellation information, please visit **brfonline.org.uk/terms**.

Bible Reading Fellowship is a charity (233280) and company limited by guarantee (301324), registered in England and Wales

ND0125

NEW DAYLIGHT GIFT SUBSCRIPTION FORM

☐ I would like to give a gift subscription (please provide both names and addresses):

Title _____ First name/initials _____ Surname _____

Address _____

_____ Postcode _____

Telephone _____ Email _____

Gift subscription name _____

Gift subscription address _____

_____ Postcode _____

Gift message (20 words max. or include your own gift card):

_____

_____

Please send *New Daylight* beginning with the May 2025 / September 2025 / January 2026 issue (*delete as appropriate*):

(*please tick box*)	UK	Europe	Rest of world
New Daylight 1-year subscription	☐ £21.30	☐ £29.55	☐ £35.25
New Daylight 3-year subscription	☐ £60.30	N/A	N/A
New Daylight Deluxe	☐ £26.55	☐ £36.00	☐ £44.10

Optional donation to support the work of BRF Ministries £ _____

Total enclosed £ _____ (cheques should be made payable to 'BRF')

Please complete and return the Gift Aid declaration on page 142 to make your donation even more valuable to us.

Please charge my MasterCard / Visa with £ _____

Card no. ☐☐☐☐ ☐☐☐☐ ☐☐☐☐ ☐☐☐☐

Expires end ☐☐☐☐ Security code ☐☐☐ Last 3 digits on the reverse of the card

We will use your personal data to process this order. From time to time we may send you information about the work of BRF Ministries. Please contact us if you wish to discuss your mailing preferences. Our privacy policy is available at **brf.org.uk/privacy**.

Please return this form with the appropriate payment to:
BRF Ministries, 15 The Chambers, Vineyard, Abingdon OX14 3FE
For terms and cancellation information, please visit **brfonline.org.uk/terms**.

Bible Reading Fellowship is a charity (233280) and company limited by guarantee (301324), registered in England and Wales

Ministries

Inspiring people of all ages to grow in Christian faith

BRF Ministries is the home of Anna Chaplaincy, Living Faith, Messy Church and Parenting for Faith

As a charity, our work would not be possible without fundraising and gifts in wills.
To find out more and to donate,
visit brf.org.uk/give or call +44 (0)1235 462305

Registered with
FUNDRAISING
REGULATOR